an Agnostic

AND OTHER ESSAYS

Clarence
Darrow

⒫ Prometheus Books

59 John Glenn Drive
Amherst, New York 14228-2197

Published 1995 by Prometheus Books
59 John Glenn Drive, Amherst, New York 14228-2197
716-691-0133. FAX: 716-691-0137

Library of Congress Cataloging-in-Publication Data

Darrow, Clarence, 1857–1938.
  Why I am an agnostic and other essays / Clarence Darrow.
      p.   cm. — (The Freethought library)
  Originally published separately by Haldeman-Julius,
Girard, Kan., beginning in 1899, in series: Little blue book.
  Contents: Why I am an agnostic — The myth of the soul —
Absurdities of the Bible — Voltaire — The skeleton in the closet.
  ISBN 0-87975-940-2 (pbk. : alk. paper)
  1. Agnosticism. 2. Darrow, Clarence, 1857–1938—Religion.
I. Title. II. Series.
BL2715.D36   1994
211′.7—dc20   94-22965
                                                      CIP

THE FREETHOUGHT LIBRARY
Featuring Selections from the Haldeman-Julius Collection

Over a period of thirty years, publisher E. Haldeman-Julius made available to millions of readers inexpensive paperback editions of classics of literature and freethought. Prometheus is proud to be reissuing selected numbers of the renowned Blue Books, *which provided a broad forum for the discussion of rationalist issues.*

Classics of Freethought
edited by Paul Blanshard

Debates on the Meaning of Life, Evolution, and Spiritualism
Frank Harris, Percy Ward, George McCready Price,
Joseph McCabe, and Sir Arthur Conan Doyle

The Forgery of the Old Testament and Other Essays
Joseph McCabe

The Militant Agnostic
E. Haldeman-Julius

The Myth of the Resurrection and Other Essays
Joseph McCabe

The Necessity of Atheism and Other Essays
Percy Bysshe Shelley

Reason, Tolerance, and Christianity: The Ingersoll Debates
Robert G. Ingersoll

The Religious Beliefs of Our Presidents
Franklin Steiner

Why I Am an Agnostic and Other Essays
Clarence Darrow

CLARENCE SEWARD DARROW was born in Kinsman, Ohio, the fifth of eight children, on April 18, 1857. Darrow's parents, who were freethinkers and abolitionists, instilled in their son a fierce independence and a devotion to learning. Following a year of study at Allegheny College in Pennsylvania, and another at the University of Michigan law school, Darrow was admitted to the Ohio bar in 1878. After practicing in Ohio for nine years, Darrow moved with his wife and son in 1887 to Chicago, where he was appointed corporation counsel to the City of Chicago and later attorney for the Chicago and North Western Railway. He resigned this position in 1894 to devote himself exclusively to labor and political cases.

Darrow became the defense lawyer in several famous trials, including those of William D. "Big Bill" Haywood, accused of a plot to assassinate the former Idaho governor, Frank B. Steunenberg (1907); of the McNamara brothers, charged with trying to blow up the Los Angeles *Times* building (1911); and of schoolteacher John Scopes, on trial in 1925 for defying the Tennessee state law forbidding the teaching of evolution. In what became known as the "Monkey" trial, Darrow's opposing counsel was William Jennings Bryan, thrice unsuccessful candidate for the Presidency and, in Darrow's eyes, the champion of religious bigotry. Applying his remarkable oratorical powers, Darrow exposed Bryan as an ignoramus and a fanatic; nevertheless, Scopes was convicted and ordered to pay a nominal fine, although the conviction was later reversed.

Darrow's philosophy was deterministic: human beings are

controlled by their feelings, emotions, and desires; this is the result of heredity and environment. Darrow rejected the concept of inherent sinfulness, arguing that people should be treated with compassion rather than with vindictiveness. A popular lecturer and writer, Darrow, in several works, including those in the Blue Book series, decried religious dogmatism and a fundamentalist interpretation of the scriptures, while upholding the values of individual liberty and social justice.

Clarence Darrow died in Chicago on March 13, 1938.

Clarence Darrow's published works include the novel *An Eye for an Eye* (1905), *Crime: Its Cause and Treatment* (1922), and *The Story of My Life* (1932).

Contents

1

Why I Am an Agnostic

An agnostic is a doubter. The word is generally applied to those who doubt the verity of accepted religious creeds or faiths. Everyone is an agnostic as to the beliefs or creeds they do not accept. Catholics are agnostic to the Protestant creeds, and the Protestants are agnostic to the Catholic creed. Anyone who thinks is an agnostic about something, otherwise he must believe that he is possessed of all knowledge. And the proper place for such a person is in the madhouse or the home for feeble-minded. In a popular way, in the Western world, an agnostic is one who doubts or disbelieves the main tenets of the Christian faith.

I would say that belief in at least three tenets is necessary to the faith of a Christian: a belief in God, a belief in immortality, and a belief in a supernatural book. Various Christian sects require much more, but it is difficult to imagine that one could be a Christian, under any intelligent meaning of the word, with less. Yet there are some people who claim to be Christians who do not accept the literal interpretation of all the Bible, and who give more credence to some portions of the book than to others.

11

I am an agnostic as to the question of God. I think that it is impossible for the human mind to believe in an object or thing unless it can form a mental picture of such object or thing. Since man ceased to worship openly an anthropomorphic God and talked vaguely and not intelligently about some Force in the universe, higher than man, that is responsible for the existence of man and the universe, he cannot be said to believe in God. One cannot believe in a force excepting as a force that pervades matter and is not an individual entity. To believe in a thing, an image of the thing must be stamped on the mind. If one is asked if he believes in such an animal as a camel, there immediately arises in his mind an image of the camel. This image has come from experience or knowledge of the animal gathered in some way or other. No such image comes, or can come, with the idea of a God who is described as a force.

Man has always speculated upon the origin of the universe, including himself. I feel, with Herbert Spencer, that whether the universe had an origin—and if it had—what the origin is will never be known by man. The Christian says that the universe could not make itself; that there must have been some higher power to call it into being. Christians have been obsessed for many years by Paley's argument that if a person passing through a desert should find a watch and examine its spring, its hands, its case and its crystal, he would at once be satisfied that some intelligent being capable of design had made the watch. No doubt this is true. No *civilized* man would question that someone made the watch. The reason he would not doubt it is because he is familiar with watches and other appliances made by man. The savage was once unfamiliar with a watch and would have had no idea upon the subject. There are plenty of crystals and rocks of natural formation that are as intricate as a watch, but even to intelligent man they carry no implication because no one has any knowledge or experience of someone having made these natural objects which everywhere abound. To say that God made the universe gives us no explanation of the beginning of things. If we are told that God made the universe, the question immediately arises: Who made God? Did he always exist, or was there some power back of that? Did he create matter out of nothing, or is his existence coextensive with matter? The problem is still there. What is the origin of it all? If, on the other hand, one says that the universe was not made by God, that it always existed, he has the same difficulty to confront. To say that the universe was here last year, or millions of years ago, does not explain its origin. This is still a mystery. As to the question of the origin of things, many can only wonder and doubt and guess.

As to the existence of the soul, all people may either believe or disbelieve. Everyone knows the origin of the human being. They know that it came from a single cell in the body of the mother, and that the cell was one out of ten thousand in the mother's body. Before gestation the cell must have been fertilized by a spermatozoon from the body of the father. This was one out of perhaps a billion spermatozoa that was the capacity of the father. When the cell is fertilized a chemical process begins. The cell divides and multiplies and increases into millions of cells, and finally a child is born. Cells die and are born during the life of the individual until they finally drop apart, and this is death.

If there is a soul, what is it, and where did it come from, and where does it go? Can anyone who is guided by his reason possibly imagine a soul independent of a body, or the place of its residence, or the character of it, or anything concerning it? If man is justified in any belief or disbelief on any subject, he is warranted in the disbelief in a soul.

Not one scrap of evidence exists to prove any such impossible thing.

Many Christians base the belief of a soul and God upon the Bible. Strictly speaking, there is no such book. To make the Bible sixty-six books are bound into one volume. These books were written by many people at different times, and no one knows the time or the identity of any author. Some of the books were written by several authors at various times. These books contain all sorts of contradictory concepts of life and morals and the origin of things. Between the first and the last nearly a thousand years intervened; a longer time than has passed since the discovery of America by Columbus.

When I was a boy the theologians used to assert that the proof of the divine inspiration of the Bible rested on miracles and prophecies. But a miracle means a violation of a natural law, and there can be no proof imagined that could be sufficient to show the violation of a natural law; even though proof seemed to show violation, it would only show that we were not acquainted with *all* natural laws. One believes in the truthfulness of a man because of his long experience with the man, and because the man has always told a consistent story. But no man has told so consistent a story as nature.

If one should say that the sun did not rise, to use the ordinary expression, on the day before, his hearer would not believe it, even though he had slept all day and knew that his informant was a man of the strictest veracity. He would not believe it because the story is inconsistent with the conduct of the sun in all the ages past.

Primitive and even civilized people have grown so accustomed to believing in miracles that they often attribute the simplest manifestation of nature to agencies of which they know nothing. They do this when the belief is utterly inconsistent with knowledge and logic. They believe in old miracles and new ones. Preachers pray for rain, knowing full well that no such prayer was ever answered. When a politician is sick, they pray for God to cure him, and the politician almost invariably dies. The modern clergyman who prays for rain and for the health of the politician is no more intelligent in this matter than the primitive man who saw a separate miracle in the rising and setting of the sun, in the birth of an individual, in the growth of a plant, in the stroke of lightning, in the flood, in every manifestation of nature and life.

As to prophecies, intelligent writers gave them up long ago. In all prophecies facts are made to suit the prophecy, or the prophecy was made after the facts, or the events have no relation to the prophecy. Weird and strange and unreasonable interpretations are used to explain simple statements, that a prophecy may be claimed.

Can any rational person believe that the Bible is anything but a human document? We now know pretty well where the various books came from, and about when they were written. We know that they were written by human beings who had no knowledge of science, little knowledge of life, and were influenced by the barbarous morality of primitive times, and were grossly ignorant of most things that men know today. For instance, Genesis says that God made the earth, and he made the sun to light the day and the moon to light the night, and in one clause disposes of the stars by saying that "he made the stars also." This was plainly written by someone who had no conception of the stars. Man, by the aid of his telescope, has looked out into the heavens and found stars whose diameter is as great as the distance between the earth and the sun. We now know that the universe is filled with stars and suns and planets and systems. Every new telescope looking further into the heavens only discovers more and more worlds and suns and systems in the endless reaches of space. The men who wrote Genesis believed, or course, that this tiny speck of mud that we call the Earth was the center of the universe, the only world in space, and made for man who was the only being worth considering. These men believed that the stars were only a little way above the earth, and were set in the firmament for man to look at, and for nothing else. Everyone today knows that this conception is not true.

The origin of the human race is not as blind a subject as it once was. Let alone God creating Adam out of hand, from the dust of the earth, does anyone believe that Eve was made from Adam's rib:—that the snake walked and spoke in the Garden of Eden—that he tempted Eve to persuade Adam to eat an apple; and that it is on that account that the whole human race was doomed to hell:—that for four thousand years there was no chance for any human to be saved, though none of them had anything whatever to do with the temptation; and that finally men were saved only through God's son dying for them, and that unless human beings believed this silly, impossible and wicked story they were doomed to hell? Can anyone with intelligence really believe that a child born today should be doomed because the snake tempted Eve and Eve tempted Adam? To believe that is not God-worship; it is devil-worship.

Can anyone call this scheme of creation and damnation moral? It defies every principle of morality, as man conceives morality. Can anyone believe today that the whole world was destroyed by flood, save only Noah and his family and a male and female of each species of animal that entered the Ark? There are almost a million species of insects alone. How did Noah match these up and make sure of getting male and female to reproduce life in the world after the flood had spent its force? And why should all the lower animals have been destroyed? Were they included in the sinning of man? This is a story which could not beguile a fairly bright child of five years of age today.

Do intelligent people believe that the various languages spoken by man on earth came from the confusion of tongues at the Tower of Babel, some four thousand years ago? Human languages were dispersed all over the face of the earth long before that time. Evidences of civilizations are in existence now that were old long before the date that romancers fix for the building of the Tower, and even before the date claimed for the flood.

Do Christians believe that Joshua made the sun stand still, so that the day could be lengthened, that a battle might be finished? What kind of person wrote that story, and what did he know about astronomy? It is perfectly plain that the author thought that the earth was the center of the universe and stood still in the heavens, and that the sun either went around it or was pulled across its path each day, and that the stopping of the sun would lengthen the day. We know now that had the sun stopped when Joshua commanded it, and had stood still until now, it would not have lengthened the day. We know that the day is determined by the rotation of the earth upon its axis, and not by the movement of the sun. Everyone knows that this story simply is not true, and not many even pretend to believe the childish fable.

What of the tale of Balaam's ass speaking to him, probably in Hebrew? Is it true, or is it a fable? Many asses have spoken, and doubtless some in Hebrew, but they have not been that breed of asses. Is salvation to depend on a belief in a monstrosity like this?

Above all the rest, would any human being today believe that a child was born without a father? Yet this story was not at all unreasonable in the ancient world; at least three or four miraculous births are recorded in the Bible, including John the Baptist, and Samson. Immaculate conceptions were common in the Roman world at the time and at the place where Christianity really had its nativity. Women were taken to the temples to be innoculated of God so that their sons might be heroes, which meant, generally, wholesale butchers. Julius Caesar was a miraculous conception—indeed they were common all over the world. How many miraculous-birth stories is a Christian now expected to believe?

In the days of the formation of the Christian religion, disease meant the possession of human beings by devils. Christ cured a sick man by casting out the devils, who ran into the swine, and the swine ran into the sea. Is there any question but that was simply the attitude and belief of a primitive people? Does anyone believe that sickness means the possession of the body by devils, and that the devils must be cast out of the human being that he may be cured? Does anyone believe that a dead person can come to life? The miracles recorded in the Bible are not the only instances of dead men coming to life. All over the world one finds testimony of such miracles; miracles which no person is expected to believe, unless it is his kind of a miracle. Still at Lourdes today, and all over the present world, from New York to Los Angeles and up and down the lands, people believe in miraculous occurrences, and even in the return of the dead. Superstition is everywhere prevalent in the world. It has been so from the beginning, and most likely will be so unto the end.

The reasons for agnosticism and skepticism are abundant and compelling. Fantastic and foolish and impossible consequences are freely claimed for the belief in religion. All the civilization of any period is put down as a result of religion. All the cruelty and error and ignorance of the period has no relation to religion. The truth is that the origin of what we call civilization is not due to religion, but to skepticism. So long as men accepted miracles without question, so long as they believed in original sin and the road to salvation— so long as they believed in a hell where man would be kept for eternity on account of Eve, there was no reason whatever for civilization; life was short, and eternity was long, and the business of life was preparation for eternity. When every event was a miracle, when there was no order or system or law, there was no occasion for studying any subject, or being interested in anything exception a religion which took care of the soul. As man doubted the primitive conceptions about religion, and no longer accepted the literal, miraculous teachings of ancient books, he set himself to understand nature. We no longer cure disease by casting out devils. Since that time, men have studied the human body, have built hospitals and treated illness in a scientific way. Science is responsible for the building of railroads and bridges, of steamships, of telegraph lines, of cities, towns, large buildings and small, plumbing and sanitation, of the food supply, and the countless thousands of useful things that we now deem necessary to life. Without skepticism and doubt, none of these things could have been given to the world.

The fear of God is not the beginning of wisdom. The fear of God is the death of wisdom. Skepticism and doubt lead to study and investigation, and investigation is the beginning of wisdom.

The modern world is the child of doubt and inquiry, as the ancient world was the child of fear and faith.

2

The Myth of the Soul

IS THE BELIEF IN IMMORTALITY
NECESSARY OR EVEN DESIRABLE?

There is, perhaps, no more striking example of the credulity of man than the widespread belief in immortality. This idea includes not only the belief that death is not the end of what we call life, but that personal identity involving memory persists beyond the grave. So determined is the ordinary individual to hold fast to this belief that, as a rule, he refuses to read or to think upon the subject lest it cast doubt upon his cherished dream. Of those who may chance to look at this contribution, many will do so with the determination not to be convinced, and will refuse even to consider the manifold reasons that might weaken their faith. I know that this is true, for I know the reluctance with which I long approached the subject and my firm determination not to give up my hope. Thus the myth will stand in the way of a sensible adjustment to facts.

Even many of those who claim to believe in immortality still tell themselves and others that neither side of the question is susceptible of proof. Just what can these hopeful ones believe that the word "proof" involves? The evidence against the persistence of personal consciousness is as strong as the evidence of gravitation, and much more obvious. It is as convincing and unassailable as the proof of the destruction of wood or coal by fire. If it is not certain that death ends personal identity and memory, then almost nothing that man accepts as true is susceptible of proof.

The beliefs of the race and its individuals are relics of the past. Without careful examination no one can begin to understand how many of man's cherished opinions have no foundation in fact. The common experience of all men should teach them how easy it is to believe, what they wish to accept. Experienced psychologists know perfectly well that if they desire to convince a man of some idea, they must first make him *want* to believe it. There are so many hopes, so many strong yearnings and desires attached to the doctrine of immortality that it is practically impossible to create in any mind the wish to be mortal. Still, in spite of strong desires, millions of people are filled with doubts and fears that will not down. After all, is it not better to look the question squarely in the face and find out whether we are harboring a delusion?

It is customary to speak of a "belief in immortality."— First, then, let us see what is meant by the word "belief." If I take a train in Chicago at noon, bound for New York, I believe I will reach that city the next morning. I believe it because I have been to New York, I have read about the city, I have known many other people who have been there, and their stories are not inconsistent with any known facts in my own experience. I have even examined the time tables and I know just how I will go and how long the trip will take. In other words, when I board the train for New York, I believe I will reach that city because I have *reason* to believe it.

If, instead, I wanted to see Timbuktu or some other point on the globe where I had never been, or of which I had only heard, I still know something about geography, and if I did not I could find out about the place I wished to visit. Through the encyclopedia and other means of information, I could get a fair idea of the location and character of the country or city, the kind of people who lived there and almost anything I wished to know, including the means of transportation and the time it would take to go and return. I already am satisfied that the earth is round, I know about its size. I know the extent of its land and water. I know the names of its countries; I know perfectly well that there are many places on its surface that I have never seen. I can easily satisfy myself as to whether there is any such place and how to get there, and what I shall do when I arrive.

But if I am told that next week I shall start on a trip to Goofville; that I shall not take my body with me; that I shall stay for all eternity: can I find a single fact connected with my journey—the way I shall go, the time of the journey, the country I shall reach, its location in space, the way I shall live there—or anything that would lead to a rational belief that I shall really make the trip? Have I ever known anyone who has made the journey and returned? If I am really to believe, I must try to get some information about all these important facts.

But people hesitate to ask questions about life after death. They do not ask, for they know that only silence comes out of the eternal darkness of endless space. If people really believed in a beautiful, happy, glorious land waiting to receive them when they died; if they believed that their friends would be waiting to meet them; if they believed that all pain and suffering would be left behind: why should they live through weeks, months, and even years of pain and torture while a cancer eats its way to the vital parts of the body? Why should one fight off death? Because he does *not* believe in any real sense; he only hopes. Everyone knows that there is no real evidence of any such state of bliss; so we are told not to search for proof. We are to accept through faith alone. But every thinking person knows that faith can only come through belief. Belief implies a condition of mind that accepts a certain idea. This condition can be brought about only by evidence. True, the evidence may be simply the unsupported statement of your grandmother; it may be wholly insufficient for reasoning men; but, good or bad, it must be enough for the believer or he could not believe.

Upon what evidence, then, are we asked to believe in immortality? There is no evidence. One is told to rely on faith, and no doubt this serves the purpose so long as one can believe blindly whatever he is told. But if there is no evidence upon which to build a positive belief in immortality, let us examine the other side of the question. Perhaps evidence can be found to support a positive conviction that immortality is a delusion.

The belief in immortality expresses itself in two different forms. On the one hand, there is a belief in the immortality of the "soul." This is sometimes interpreted to mean simply that the identity, the consciousness, the memory of the individual persists after death. On the other hand, many religious creeds formulated a belief in "the resurrection of the body"—which is something else again. It will be necessary to examine both forms of this belief in turn.

The idea of continued life after death is very old. It doubtless had its roots back in the childhood of the race. In view of the limited knowledge of primitive man, it was not unreasonable. His dead friends and relatives visited him in dreams and visions and were present in his feeling and imagination until they were forgotten. Therefore, the lifeless body did not raise the question of dissolution, but rather of duality. It was thought that man was a dual being possessing a body and a soul as separate entities, and that when a man died, his soul was released from his body to continue its life apart. Consequently, food and drink were placed upon the graves of the dead to be used in the long journey into the unknown. In modified forms, this belief in the duality of man persists to the present day. But primitive man had no conception of life as having a beginning and an end. In this he was like the rest of the animals. Today, everyone of ordinary intelligence knows how life begins, and to examine the beginnings of life leads to inevitable conclusions about the way life ends. If man has a soul, it must creep in somewhere during the period of gestation and growth.

All the higher forms of animal life grow from a single cell. Before the individual life can begin its development, it must be fertilized by union with another cell; then the cell divides and multiplies until it takes the form and pattern of its kind. At a certain regular time the being emerges into the world. During its term of life millions of cells in its body are born, die, and are replaced until, through age, disease, or some catastrophe, the cells fall apart and the individual life is ended.

It is obvious that but for the fertilization of the cell under right conditions, the being would not have lived. It is idle to say that the initial cell has a soul. In one sense it has life; but even that is precarious and depends for its continued life upon union with another cell of the proper kind. The human mother is the bearer of probably ten thousand of one kind of cell, and the human father of countless billions of the other kind. Only a very small fraction of these result in human life. If the unfertilized cells of the female and the unused cells of the male are human beings possessed of souls, then the population of the world is infinitely greater than has ever been dreamed. Of course no such idea as belief in the immortality of the germ cells could satisfy the yearnings of the individual for a survival of life after death.

If that which is called a "soul" is a separate entity apart from the body, when, then, and where and how was this soul placed in the human structure? The individual began with the union of two cells, neither of which had a soul. How could these two soulless cells produce a soul? I must leave this search to the metaphysicians. When they have found the answer, I hope they will tell me, for I should really like to know.

We know that a baby may live and fully develop in its mother's womb and then, through some shock at birth, may be born without life. In the past, these babies were promptly buried. But now we know that in many such cases, where the bodily structure is complete, the machine may be set to work by artificial respiration or electricity. Then it will run like any other human body through its allotted term of years. We also know that in many cases of drowning, or when some mishap virtually destroys life without hopelessly impairing the body, artificial means may set it in motion once more, so that it will complete its term of existence until the final catastrophe comes. Are we to believe that somewhere around the stillborn child and somewhere in the vicinity of the drowned man there hovers a detached soul waiting to be summoned back into the body by a pulmotor? This, too, must be left to the metaphysicians.

The beginnings of life yield no evidence of the beginnings of a soul. It is idle to say that the something in the human being which we call "life" is the soul itself, for the soul is generally taken to distinguish human beings from other forms of life. There is life in all animals and plants, and at least potential life in inorganic matter. This potential life is simply unreleased force and matter—the great storehouse from which all forms of life emerge and are constantly replenished. It is impossible to draw the line between inorganic matter and the simpler forms of plant life, and equally impossible to draw the line between plant life and animal life, or between other forms of animal life and what we human beings are pleased to call the highest form. If the thing which we call "life" is itself the soul, then cows have souls; and, in the very nature of things, we must allow souls to all forms of life and to inorganic matter as well.

Life itself is something very real, as distinguished from the soul. Every man knows that his life had a beginning. Can one imagine an organism that has a beginning and no end? If I did not exist in the infinite past, why should I, or could I, exist in the infinite future? "But," say some, "your consciousness, your memory may exist even after you are dead. This is what we mean by the soul." Let us examine this point a little.

I have no remembrance of the months that I lay in my mother's womb. I cannot recall the day of my birth nor the time when I first opened my eyes to the light of the sun. I cannot remember when I was an infant, or when I began to creep on the floor, or when I was taught to walk, or anything before I was five or six years old. Still, all of these events were important, wonderful, and strange in a new life. What I call my "consciousness," for lack of a better word and a better understanding, developed with my growth and the crowding experiences I met at every turn. I have a hazy recollection of the burial of a boy soldier who was shot toward the end of the Civil War. He was buried near the schoolhouse when I was seven years old. But I have no remembrance of the assassination of Abraham Lincoln, although I must then have been eight years old. I must have known about it at the time, for my family and my community idolized Lincoln, and all America was in mourning at his death. Why do I remember the dead boy soldier who was buried a year before? Perhaps because I knew him well. Perhaps because his family was close to my childish life. Possibly because it came to me as my first knowledge of death. At all events, it made so deep an impression that I recall it now.

"Ah, yes," say the believers in the soul, "what you say confirms our own belief. You certainly existed when these early experiences took place. You were conscious of them at the time, even though you are not aware of it now. In the same way, may not your consciousness persist after you die, even though you are not aware of the fact?"

On the contrary, my fading memory of the events that filled the early years of my life leads me to the opposite conclusion. So far as these incidents are concerned, the mind and consciousness of the boy are already dead. Even now, am I fully alive? I am seventy-one years old. I often fail to recollect the names of some of those I knew full well. Many events do not make the lasting impression that they once did. I know that it will be only a few years, even if my body still survives decay, when few important matters will even register in my mind. I know how it is with the old. I know that physical life can persist beyond the time when the mind can fully function. I know that if I live to an extreme old age, may mind will fail. I shall eat and drink and go to my bed in an automatic way. Memory—which is all that binds me to the past—will already be dead. All that will remain will be a vegetative existence; I shall sit and doze in the chimney corner, and my body will function in a measure even though the ego will already be practically dead. I am sure that if I die of what is called "old age," my consciousness will gradually slip away with my failing emotions! I shall no more be aware of the near approach of final dissolution than is the dying tree.

I am aware that now and then at long intervals there is a man who preserves his faculties until a late period of his life. I know that these cases are very, very rare. No superstition needs to be called into service to account for the unusual things that are incident to life. There may be those who retain, in a measurable degree, consciousness and mental activity beyond the time of the ordinary mortal. Still, everyone with the least information knows that it is almost a universal rule that the body declines with age, and that those who live a long life gradually yield their intellectual activity until they reach the period of senility and unconsciousness.

In primitive times, before men knew anything about the human body or the universe of which it is a part, it was not unreasonable to believe in spirits, ghosts, and the duality of man. For one thing, celestial geography was much simpler then. Just above the earth was a firmament in which the stars were set, and above the firmament was heaven. The place was easy of access and in dreams the angels were seen going up and coming down on a ladder. But now we have a slightly more adequate conception of space and the infinite universe of which we are so small a part. Our great telescopes reveal countless worlds and planetary systems which make our own sink into utter insignificance in comparison. We have every reason to think that beyond our sight there is endless space filled with still more planets, so infinite in size and number that no brain has the smallest conception of their extent. Is there any reason to think that in this universe, with its myriads of worlds, there is no other life so important as our own? Is it possible that the inhabitants of the earth have been signaled out for special favor and endowed with souls and immortal life? Is it at all reasonable to suppose that any special account is taken of the human atoms that forever come and go upon this planet?

If man has a soul that persists after death, that goes to a heaven of the blessed or to a hell of the damned, where are these places? It is not so easily imagined as it once was. How does the soul make its journey? What does immortal man find when he gets there, and how will he live after he reaches the end of endless space? We know that the atmosphere will be absent; that there will be no light, no heat—only the infinite reaches of darkness and frigidity.

If there is a future place for the abode of the spirits of the dead, where is this place? Trusting people have made pictures and mental images of this abode of the dead. The revelation of St. John treats rather specifically of this far-off land, but it is evident that St. John was a psychopath and his case would be plainly recognized today. True, this picture of St. John's is not very alluring to intelligent men. Still, trusting and confiding mortals have visioned in words, at least, a land where families would be reunited and neighbors and friends come together once more. In this smug little place, fashioned upon experiences of life upon this mundane sphere, husbands and wives, long parted, will be united. Parents and children, and grandparents and grandchildren, too, will assemble in families in that land of the blessed and the dead.

These conceptions were formed early in the history of man; in fact, it has only been in recent years that we have had any knowledge or vision of the immensity of space and of the impossibility of any such place as is visioned by the credulous and trusting. We know now that the earth revolves upon its axis at a terrific speed. This motion makes a complete revolution in twenty-four hours. We know down to the second of time that no spot bears the same relation to space as it did before. If one who dies at midnight has a soul and starts on his trip to Heaven, he goes in an opposite direction from one who dies at noon, and the chances to meet under any circumstances which can be conceived would grow less as they traveled on. Besides this revolution on its axis, the earth is traveling at an inconceivable speed around the sun, which, at times, is about ninety-three million miles away. This complete journey is made once a year. In its orbit around the sun it travels more than a thousand miles a minute. This constant appalling speed would evidently add to the confusion of two mortals locating themselves in the same spot in space, even though they had souls. The atmosphere, even in its most attenuated form, does not reach over five hundred miles away from the earth, and for only a small fraction of that space could life as we conceive it exist. And when the earth leaves a given spot in space the atmosphere is carried along with it. In addition to the motion of the earth on its axis and its unthinkable speed in its circuit around the sun, the whole solar system is traveling around the pole star, accompanied no doubt by many other systems like our own; no one can tell how fast it goes or how far it goes, in what seems endless space. And these systems travel in turn around some other centra point in the far-off Milky Way, and no one knows how many other apparently central points some where off amongst the stars and worlds and suns furnish foci around which the earth and all the systems constantly revolve. What possible means of locomotion could be furnished for mortals to find a place of rest, and what possible unimaginable guide could pilot individuals going in different directions at all times of the day and night and all portions of the year and century, and other greater periods of time, to this haven of the blessed? All of these conceptions beggar any sort of imagination and make and substitute the wildest unthinkable dreams in place of real beliefs.

There are those who base their hope of a future life upon the resurrection of the body. This is a purely religious doctrine. It is safe to say that few intelligent men who are willing to look obvious facts in the face hold any such belief. Yet we are seriously told that Elijah was carried bodily to heaven in a chariot of fire, and that Jesus arose from the dead and ascended into heaven. The New Testament abounds in passages that support this doctrine. St. Paul states the tenet over and over again. In the fifteenth chapter of first Corinthians he says: "If Christ be preached that he rose from the dead, how say some among you that there is no resurrection of the dead? . . . And if Christ be not risen, then is our preaching vain. . . . For if the dead rise not, then is not Christ raised." The Apostles' Creed says: "I believe in the resurrection of the body." This has been carried into substantially all the orthodox creeds; and while it is more or less minimized by neglect and omission, it is still a cardinal doctrine of the orthodox churches.

Two thousand years ago, in Palestine, little was known of man, of the earth, or of the universe. It was then currently believed that the earth was only four thousand years old, that life had begun anew after the deluge about two thousand years before, and that the entire earth was soon to be destroyed. Today it is fairly well established that man has been upon the earth for a million years. During that long stretch of time the world has changed many times; it is changing every moment. At least three or four ice ages have swept across continents, driving death before them, carrying human beings into the sea or burying them deep in the earth. Animals have fed on man and on each other. Every dead body, no matter whether consumed by fire or buried in the earth, has been resolved into its elements, so that the matter and energy that once formed human beings has fed animals and plants and other men. As the great naturalist, Fabre, has said: "At the banquet of life each is in turn a guest and a dish." This the body of every man now living is in part made from the bodies of those who have been dead for ages.

Yet we are still asked to believe in the resurrection of the body. By what alchemy, then, are the individual bodies that have successfully fed the generations of men to be separated and restored to their former identities? And if I am to be resurrected, what particular *I* shall be called from the grave, from the animals and plants and the bodies of other men who shall inherit this body I now call my own? My body has been made over and over, piece by piece, as the days went by, and will continue to be so made until the end. It has changed so slowly that each new cell is fitted into the living part, and will go on changing until the final crisis comes. Is it the child in the mother's womb or the tottering frame of the old man that shall be brought back? The mere thought of such a resurrection beggars reason, ignores facts, and enthrones blind faith, wild dreams, hopeless hopes, and cowardly fears as sovereign of the human mind.

Some of those who profess to believe in the immortality of man—whether it be of his soul or his body—have drawn what comfort they could from the modern scientific doctrine of the indestructibility of matter and force. This doctrine, they say, only confirms in scientific language what they have always believed. This, however, is pure sophistry. If is probably true that no matter or force has ever been or ever can be destroyed. But it is likewise true that there is no connection whatever between the notion that personal consciousness and memory persist after death and the scientific theory that matter and force are indestructible. For the scientific theory carries with it a corollary, that the forms of matter and energy are constantly changing through an endless cycle of new combinations. Of what possible use would it be, then, to have a consciousness that was immortal, but which, from the moment of death, was dispersed into new combinations, so that no two parts of the original identity could ever be reunited again?

These natural processes of change, which in the human being take the forms of growth, disease, senility, death, and decay, are essentially the same as the processes by which a lump of coal is disintegrated in burning. One may watch the lump of coal burning in the grate until nothing but ashes remains. Part of the coal goes up the chimney in the form of smoke; part of it radiates through the house as heat; the residue lies in the ashes on the hearth. So it is with human life. In all forms of life nature is engaged in combining, breaking down, and recombining her store of energy and matter into new forms. The thing we call "life" is nothing other than a state of equilibrium which endures for a short span of years between the two opposing tendencies of nature—the one that builds up, and the one that tears down. In old age, the tearing-down process has already gained the ascendency, and when death intervenes, the equilibrium is finally upset by the complete stoppage of the building-up process, so that nothing remains but complete disintegration. The energy thus released may be converted into grass or trees or animal life; or it may lie dormant until caught up again in the crucible of nature's laboratory. But whatever happens, the man—the *You* and the *I*—like the lump of coal that has been burned, is gone—irrevocably dispersed. All the King's horses and all the King's men cannot restore it to its former unity.

The idea that man is a being set apart, distinct from all the rest of nature, is born of man's emotions, of his loves and hates, of his hopes and fears, and of the primitive conceptions of undeveloped minds. The *You* and the *I* which is known to our friends does not consist of an immaterial something called a "soul" which cannot be conceived. We know perfectly well what we mean when we talk about this *You* and this *Me*: and it is equally plain that the whole fabric that makes up our separate personalities is destroyed, dispersed, disintegrated beyond repair by what we call "death."

As a matter of fact, does *anyone* really believe in a future life? The faith does not simply involve the persistence of activity, but it has been stretched and magnified to mean a future world infinitely better than the earth. In this far-off land no troubles will harass the body or the soul. Eternity will be an eternity of bliss. Heaven, a land made much more delightful because of the union with those who have gone before. This doctrine has been taught so persistently through the years that men and women of strong faith in their dying moments have seen relatives and friends, long since dead, who have come to lead them to their heavenly home.

Does the conduct of the intense disciple show that he really believes that death is a glad deliverance? Why do men and women who are suffering torture on earth seek to prolong their days of agony? Why do victims of cancer being slowly eaten alive for months and years prefer enduring such pain rather than going to a land of bliss? Why will the afflicted travel all over the world and be cut to pieces by inches that they may stay a few weeks longer, in agony and torture? The one answer that is made to this query is that the afflicted struggle to live because it is their duty to hang fast to mortal life, no matter what the pain or the expected joy in heaven. The answer is not true. The afflicted cling to life because they doubt their faith, and do not wish to let go of what they have, terrible as it is.

Those who refuse to give up the idea of immortality declare that nature never creates a desire without providing the means for its satisfaction. They likewise insist that all people, from the rudest to the most civilized, yearn for another life. As a matter of fact, nature creates many desires which she does not satisfy; most of the wishes of men meet no fruition. But nature does not create any emotion demanding a future life. The only yearning that the individual has is to keep on living—which is a very different thing. This urge is found in every animal, in every plant. It is simply the momentum of a living structure: or, as Schopenhauer put it, "the will to live." What we long for is a continuation of our present state of existence, not an uncertain reincarnation in a mysterious world of which we know nothing. The idea of another life is created after men are convinced that this life ends.

I am not unmindful of those who base their hope of a future life on what they claim are the evidences furnished by the investigation of spiritualism. So far as having any prejudice against this doctrine, I have no more desire to disbelieve than I have as to any other theories of a future life. In fact, for many years, I have searched here for evidence that man still lives after all our senses show that he is dead. For more than fifty years until almost ten years past, I have given some attention to spiritualism. I have read most of the important books of scientists: Alfred Russel Wallace, Crooks, Oliver Lodge, and the books of many other men of ability and integrity who believed that they had found their dead friends who had come back to them. Likewise, I have for years investigated what are called spiritual phenomena. I am satisfied that if any intelligent man, in possession of his senses, thoroughly investigates spiritualism, he will find that there is no evidence to support his faith. At least nine-tenths of the phenomena can be set down as pure fraud and imposition. The evidence comes in the main from mediums who are ignorant, and whose tricks are clumsy in the extreme. Perhaps one-tenth of the manifestations are not the result of fraud but the evidence is entirely inadequate to prove the cause of the phenomena. It is possible that there are phenomena which no one can explain. I have many times seen what are called manifestations of spirit-return that I could not explain, but all of these failed utterly to convince me of the communication of disembodied spirits. It does not follow that because the manifestations are strange and weird, and for the present unexplainable, that those phenomena show that life persists after death. In the realm of these manifestations, the evidence of scientists is worth no more than the evidence of other men. Most likely it is worth much less. The truth is that real scientists, outside of their special field, are more helpless than other men in detecting frauds and tricks. It is likewise true that most of the men of science, like Sir Oliver Lodge, have come to their conviction late in life, and under some great stress, which is calculated to unsettle the mind, in the particular field to which they appeal.

Sir Oliver Lodge lost his son in the great war [World War I]. This was a sore bereavement to this eminent scientist. When one considers the greatness of Lodge, the clearness with which he discusses every scientific theory with which he deals, and then reads his book called *Raymond,* in which he tells of his meetings with his beloved son, it is not difficult to see that as to this bereavement his mind was unsettled and he is reaching out in the darkness to find what he so strongly wants.

Is it possible that any sort of proof could prove the existence of an individual after his decay? Suppose that some good fairy, distressed at my unbelief, should come to me with the offer to produce any evidence that I desired to satisfy me that I would see my loved ones after death; suppose I should tell this fairy that my father had been dead for twenty years; that I followed his lifeless body to the crematory where he was converted into ashes; that I desired to have him brought back to me as a living entity, and to stay in my house for a year, that I might not be deceived. Assume that when the year had passed I should go out and tell my neighbors and friends that my father had been living in my house, although he died two score years ago; suppose that they believed implicitly in my integrity and my judgment; even then, could I convince one person that my statement was true? Would they be right in doubting my word? After all, which is the more reasonable, that the dead have come back to life, or that I have become insane? All of my friends would say: "Poor fellow, I am sorry he has lost his mind." Against the universal experience of mankind and nature, the dementia or the insanity of one man, or a thousand men, could count as nothing. The insane asylums of the world are filled with men who have these dreams and visions which are realities to them, but which no one else believes, because they are entirely at variance with well-known facts.

All men recognize the hopelessness of finding any evidence that the individual will persist beyond the grave. As a last resort, we are told that it is better that the doctrine be believed even if it is not true. We are assured that without this faith, life is only desolation and despair. However that may be, it remains that many of the conclusions of logic are not pleasant to contemplate; still, so long as men think and feel, at least some of them will use their faculties as best they can. For if we are to believe things that are not true, who is to write our creed? Is it safe to leave it to any man or organization to pick out the errors that we must accept? The whole history of the world has answered this question in a way that cannot be mistaken.

And after all, is the belief in immortality necessary or even desirable for man? Millions of men and women have no such faith; they go on with their daily tasks and feel joy and sorrow without the lure of immortal life. The things that really affect the happiness of the individual are the matters of daily living. They are the companionship of friends, the games and contemplations. They are misunderstandings and cruel judgments, false friends and debts, poverty and disease. They are our joys in our living companions and our sorrows over those who die. Whatever our faith, we mainly live in the present—in the here and now. Those who hold the view that man is mortal are never troubled by metaphysical problems. At the end of the day's labor we are glad to lose our consciousness in sleep; and intellectually, at least, we look forward to the long rest from the stresses and storms that are always incidental to existence.

When we fully understand the brevity of life, its fleeting joys and unavoidable pains; when we accept the facts that all men and women are approaching an inevitable doom: the consciousness of it should make us more kindly and considerate of each other. This feeling should make men and women use their best efforts to help their fellow travelers on the road, to make the path brighter and easier as we journey on. It should bring a closer kinship, a better understanding, and a deeper sympathy for the wayfarers who must live a common life and die a common death.

3

Absurdities of the Bible

Why am I an agnostic? Because I don't believe some of the things that other people say they believe. Where do you get your religion, anyway? I don't bother to discuss just what religion is, but I think a fair definition of religion could take account of two things, at least, immortality and God, and that both of them are based on some book, so practically all of it is a book.

As I have neither the time nor the learning to discuss every religious book on earth, and as I live in Chicago, I am interested in the Christian religion. So I will discuss the book that deals with the Christian religion. Is the Bible the work of anything but man? Of course, there is no such book as the Bible. The Bible is made up of sixty-six books, some of them written by various authors at various times, covering a period of about 1,000 years—all the literature that they could find over a period longer than the time that has elapsed since the discovery of America down to the present time.

Is the Bible anything but a human book? Of course, those who are believers take both sides of it. If there is anything that troubles them, "We don't believe this." Anything that doesn't trouble them they do believe.

What about its accounts of the origin of the world? What about its account of the first man and the first woman? Adam was the first, made about less than 6,000 years ago. Well, of course, every scientist knows that human beings have been on the earth at least a half-million years, probably more. Adam got lonesome and they made a companion for him. That was a good day's work—or a day's work anyhow.

FROM RIB TO WOMAN

They took a simple way to take one of Adam's ribs and cut it out and make it into a woman.

Now, is that story a fact or a myth? How many preachers would say it was a myth? None! There are some people who still occupy Christian pulpits who say it is, but they used to send them to the stake for that.

If it isn't true then, what is? How much did they know about science in those days, how much did they know about the heavens and the earth? The earth was flat, or did God write that down, or did the old Hebrew write it down because he didn't know any better and nobody else then knew any better?

What was the heavens? The sun was made to light the day and the moon to light the night. The sun was pulled out in the day time and taken in at night and the moon was pulled across after the sun was taken out. I don't know what they did in the dark of the moon. They must have done something.

The stars, all there is about the stars, "the stars he made also." They were just "also."

Did the person who wrote that know anything whatever about astronomy? Not a thing. They believed they were just little things up in the heavens, in the firmament, just a little way above the earth, about the size of a diamond in an alderman's shirt stud. They always believed it until astronomers came along and told them something different.

Adam and Even were put in a garden where everything was lovely and there were no weeds to hoe down. They were allowed to stay there on one condition, and that is that they didn't eat of the tree of knowledge. That has been the condition of the Christian church from then until now. They haven't eaten as yet, as a rule they do not.

They were expelled from the garden, Eve was tempted by the snake who presumably spoke to her in Hebrew. And she fell for it and of course Adam fell for it, and then they were driven out. How many believe that story today?

If the Christian church doesn't believe it why doesn't it say so? You do not find them saying that. If they do not believe it here and there, someone says it. That is, he says it at great danger to his immortal soul, to say nothing of his good standing in his church.

The snake was cursed to go on his belly after that. How he went before, the story doesn't say. And Adam was cursed to work. That is why we have to work. That is, some of us—not I.

And Eve and all of her daughters to the end of time were condemned to bring forth children in pain and agony. Lovely God, isn't it? Lovely!

CAN'T BELIEVE STORY

If that story was necessary to keep me out of hell and put me in heaven—necessary for my life—I wouldn't believe it because I couldn't believe it.

I do not think any God could have done it and I wouldn't worship a God who would. It is contrary to every sense of justice that we know anything about.

God had a great deal of trouble with the earth after he made it. People were building a tower—the Tower of Babel—so that they could go up and peek over.

God didn't want them to do that and so he confounded their tongues. A man would call up for a pail of mortar and they would send him up a tub of suds, or something like that. They couldn't understand each other.

Is that true? How did they happen to right it? They found there were various languages, and that is the origin of the languages. Everybody knows better today.

Is that story true? Did God write it? He must have known; he must have been all-knowing then as he is all-knowing now.

I do not need to mention them. You remember that joy-ride that Balaam was taking on the ass. That was the only means of locomotion they had besides walking. It is the only one pretty near that they have now. Balaam wanted to get along too fast and he was beating the ass and the ass turned around and asked him what he was doing it for. In Hebrew, of course. It must have been in Hebrew for Balaam was a Jew.

And Joshua Said to the Sun, "Stand Still."

Is that true or is it a story?

And Joshua; you remember about Joshua. He was a great general. Very righteous and he was killing a lot of people and he hadn't quite finished the job and so he turned to the mountain top and said to the sun, "Stand still till I finish this job," and it stood still.

Is that one of the true ones or one of the foolish ones?

There are several things that that does. It shows how little they knew about the earth and day and night. Of course, they thought that if the sun stood still it wouldn't be pulled along any further and the night wouldn't come on. We know that if it had stood still from that day to this it wouldn't have affected the day or night; that is affected by the revolution of the earth on its axis.

Is it true? Am I wicked bacause I know it cannot possibly be true? Have you got to get rid of all your knowledge and all your common sense to save your soul?

Wait until I am a little older; maybe I can then. But my friend says that he doesn't believe those stories. They are figurative.

Are they figurative? Then what about the New Testament? Why does he believe these stories?

Here was a child born of a virgin. What evidence is there?

'TWAS THE FASHION

What evidence? Do you suppose you could get any positive evidence that would make anyone believe that story today or anybody, no matter who it was?

Child, born of a virgin! There were at least four miraculous births recorded in the Testament. There was Sarah's child, there was Samson, there was John the Baptist, and there was Jesus. Miraculous births were rather a fashionable thing in those days, especially in Rome, where most of the theology was laid out.

Caesar had a miraculous birth, Cicero, Alexander from

Macedonia—nobody was in style or great unless he had a miraculous birth. It was a land of miracles.

What evidence is there of it? How much evidence would it require for intelligent people to believe such a story? It wouldn't be possible to bring evidence anywhere in this civilized land today, right under your own noses. Nobody would believe it anyway, and yet some people say that you must believe that without a scintilla of evidence of any sort.

Jesus had brothers and sisters older than Himself. His genealogy by Matthew is traced to his father, Joseph, in the first chapter of Matthew. Read that. What did he do?

Well, now, probably some of his teachings were good. We have heard about the Sermon on the Mount. There isn't a single word contained in the Sermon on the Mount that isn't contained in what is called the Sacred Book of the Jews, long before He lived—not one single thing.

Jesus was an excellent student of Jewish theology, as anybody can tell by reading the Gospels; every bit of it was taken from their books of authority, and He simply said what He had heard of for years and years.

But let's look at some things charged to Him. He walked on the water. Now how does that sound? Do you suppose Jesus walked on the water? Joe Smith tried it when he established the Mormon religion. What evidence have you of that?

He found some of His disciples fishing and they hadn't gotten a bite all day. Jesus said, "Cast your nets down there," and they drew them in full of fish. The East Indians couldn't do better than that. What evidence is there of it?

He was at a performance where there were 5,000 people and they were out of food, and He asked them how much they had; five loaves and three fishes, or three fishes and five loaves, or something like that, and He made the five loaves and three fishes feed all the multitude and they picked up I don't know how many barrels afterward. Think of that.

How does that commend itself to intelligent people, coming from a land of myth and fable as all Asia was, a land of myth and fable and ignorance in the main, and before anybody knew anything about science? And yet that must be believed—and is—to save us from our sins.

What are these sins? What has the human race done that was so bad, except to eat of the tree of knowledge? Does anybody need to save man from his sins in a miraculous way? It is an absurd piece of theology which they themselves say that you must accept on faith because your reason won't lead you to it. You can't do it that way.

WE MUST DEVELOP REASON

I know the weakness of human reason, other people's reason. I know the weakness of it, but it is all we have, and the only safety of man is to cultivate it and extend his knowledge so that he will be sure to understand life and as many of the mysteries of the universe as he can possibly solve.

Jesus practiced medicine without medicine. Now think of this one. He was traveling along the road and somebody came and told Him there was a sick man in the house and he wanted Him to cure him. How did He do it? Well, there were a lot of hogs out in the front yard and He drove the devils out of a man and cured him, but He drove them into the hogs and they jumped into the sea. Is that a myth or is it true?

If that is true, if you have got to believe that story in order to have your soul saved, you are bound to get rid of your intelligence to save the soul that perhaps doesn't exist at all. You can't believe a thing just because you want to believe it and you can't believe it on very poor evidence. You may believe it because your grandfather told you it was true, but you have got to have some such details.

Did He raise a dead man to life? Why, tens of thousands of dead men and women have been raised to life according to all the stories and all the traditions. Was this the only case? All Europe is filled with miracles of that sort, the Catholic church performing miracles almost to the present time. Does anybody believe it if they use their senses? I say, No. It is impossible to believe it if you use your senses.

Now take the soul. People in this world instinctively like to keep on living. They want to meet their friends again, and all of that. They cling to life. Schopenhauer called it the will to live. I call it the momentum of a going machine. Anything that is going keeps on going for a certain length of time. It is all momentum. What evidence is there that we are alive after we are dead?

But that wasn't the theory of theology. The theory of theology—and it is a part of a creed of practically every Christian church today—is that you die and go down into the earth and you are dead, and when Gabriel comes back to blow his horn, the dust is gathered together and, lo and behold, you appear the same old fellow again and live here on earth!

How many believe it? And yet that is the only idea of immortality that there is, and it is in every creed today, I believe.

MATTER INDESTRUCTIBLE

And everything that is in the body and in the man goes into something else, turns into the crucible of nature, goes to make trees and grass and weeds and fruit, and is eaten by all kinds of life, and in that way goes on and on.

Of course, in a sense, nobody dies. The matter that is in me will exist in another form when I am dead. The force that is in me will live in some other kind of force when I am dead. But I will be gone.

That isn't the kind of immortality people want. They want to know that they can recognize Mary Jane in heaven. Don't they? They want to see their brothers and their sisters and their friends in heaven. It isn't possible. We know where our life began; we know where it ends.

We know where every individual life on earth began. It began in a single cell, in the body of our mother, who had some 10,000 of those cells. It was fertilized by a spermatozoon from the body of our father, who had a million of them, any one of which, under certain circumstances, would fertilize a cell.

They multiplied and divided until a child was born. And in old age or accident or disease, they fall apart and the man is done.

AGNOSTIC BECAUSE I MUST REASON

Can you imagine an eternity with one end cut off? Something that began but never ended? We began our immortality at a certain time, when the cell and the spermatozoon conspired to form a human being. We began then. If I am not the product of a spermatozoon and a cell, and if those cells which are unfertilized produce life, and those spermatozoa that fertilized no life were still alive, then I must have 10,000 brothers and sisters on my mother's side and a million on my father's. It is utterly absurd.

Now I am not a revivalist. In fact, I am not interested. I am asked to say why I am an agnostic. I am an agnostic because I trust my reason. It may not be the greatest that ever existed. I am inclined to admit that it isn't. But it is the best I have. That is a mighty sight better than some other people's at that.

I am an agnostic because no man living can form any picture of any God, and you can't believe in an object unless you can form a picture of it. You may believe in the force, but not in the object.

If there is any God in the universe I don't know it. Some people say they know it instinctively. Well, the errors and foolish things that men have known instinctively are so many we can't talk about them.

As a rule, the less a person knows, the surer he is, and he gets it by instinct, and it can't be disputed, for I don't know what is going on in another man's mind. I have no such instinct.

Let me give you just one more idea of a miracle of this Jesus story which has run down through the ages and is not at all the sole property of the Christian.

You remember, when Jesus was born in a manger, according to the story, there came wise men from the east to Jerusalem. And they were led by a star.

Now the closest star to the earth is more than a billion miles away. Think of the star leading three moth-eaten camels to a manger! Can you imagine a star standing over any house?

Can you imagine a star standing over the earth even?

What will they say, if they had time? That was a miracle. It came down to the earth.

Well, if any star came that near the earth or anywhere near the earth, it would immediately disarrange the whole solar system. Anybody who can believe those old myths and fables isn't governed by reason.

4

Voltaire

Voltaire was born in Paris in 1694. At that time, Louis XIV was on the throne in France. Through long years of profligacy and dissipation the lords and rulers of France had reduced the country to poverty and the people to slavery and superstition. France was nothing but the king and the favorites of the court. Noblemen, priests and women of easy virtue were the rulers, and people lived only to furnish them amusement and dissipation. Everyone believed in miracles, witchcraft and revealed religion. They not only believed in old miracles but in new ones. A person may be intellectual and believe in miracles, but the miracles must be very old.

Doctors plied their trade through sorcery and sacred charms. Lawyers helped keep the poor in subjection; the criminal code was long, cruel and deadly. The priest, the doctor and the lawyer lived for the rich and helped make slaves of the poor. Doctors still believe in sorcery, but they administer their faith cures through a bottle instead of vulgar witchcraft. Lawyers still keep the poor in their place by jails and barbarous laws, but the criminal code is shorter and less severe.

When Voltaire was born there was really but one church

which, of course, was ignorant, tyrannical and barbarous in the extreme. All creeds are alike, and whenever there is but one, and the rulers honestly believe in that one, they are bound to be ignorant, barbarous and cruel. All sorts of heresies were punishable by death. If anyone dared to write a pamphlet or book that questioned any part of the accepted faith, the book was at once consigned to flames and the author was lucky if he did not meet the same fate. Religion was not maintained by the precepts of the priest, but by the prison, the torture chamber and the fagot. Everyone believed; no one questioned. The religious creeds, while strict and barbarous, did not interfere with the personal conduct of any of the rulers. They were left free to act as they pleased, so long as they professed to believe in the prevailing faith.

France was on the verge of bankruptcy. Her possessions were dwindling away. There was glitter and show and extravagance on the outside; poverty, degredation and ignorance beneath. It was in this state and at that time that Voltaire was born. He was a puny child, whom no one thought would live. The priest was called in immediately that he might be baptized so his soul would be saved.

Voltaire's father was a notary of mediocre talents and some property, but his name would have been lost, excepting for his brilliant son. His mother was his mother, and that was all. In his writings, the most voluminous ever left by any author, he scarcely mentions his mother a half dozen times. He had a brother and sister whose names have only been rescued from oblivion by the luster of Voltaire. No one can find in any of his ancestors or kin, any justification for the genius of Voltaire.

Had the modern professors of eugenics had power in France in 1694, they probably would not have permitted such a child to have been born. Their scientific knowledge would have shown conclusively that no person of value could have come from the union of his father and mother. In those days, nature had not been instructed by the professors of eugenics and so Voltaire was born.

In a few days, his parents and nurse grew tired of waiting for him to die, and while he was yet a child, his education was left in charge of a priest named Chateauneuf. His teacher drew a salary as a priest, but was irreligious, profligate, clever and skeptical in the extreme. He was kind-hearted and good-natured and fond of his pupil, who was also his godson, and did his best to keep the young mind free from the superstition of the age.

Before he was ten years old, it was plain that the young Voltaire had a clever mind. At that age he was sent to a boys' school in France. His body was lean and thin and his mind was keen and active, and neither his body nor his mind changed these characteristics to the day of his death. At the school he says he learned "Latin and nonsense," and nothing else. In two hundred years, the schools are still teaching Latin and nonsense. The course of Latin is the same, but the kinds of nonsense have somewhat changed. At the school he was not like the other boys. He did not care for games or sports. While the other children were busy with youthful games he was talking with the fathers, who were the teachers in the school. In vain they tried to make the boy join the rest in play. He turned his eyes to his professors and said, "Everyone must jump after his own fashion." One of the professors, who was close to him, remarked, "That boy wants to weigh the great questions of the day in his little scales."

While a boy at school he began to write verses, not, of course, the easy, fluent, witty poetry of his later years, but still verses of such promise and originality as to attract the attention of his teachers. The one father who disliked him at school, in answering a brilliant retort of the child, said, "Witch, you will one day be the standard bearer of Deism in France."

On his return from school, about fifteen, his father decided to make him an advocate. He picked out the profession for his son, as most fathers do, because it was his own; but Voltaire's early efforts at poetry had given him the ambition to write and he insisted that he should not follow his father's footsteps, but devote his life to literature. This his father would not consent to. "Literature," said the parent, "is the profession of the man who wishes to be useless to society, a burden to his relatives, and to die of hunger." But even Voltaire's father could not make a lawyer out of a genius. To be a good lawyer, one must have a mind and a disposition to venerate the past; a respect for precedents; believe in the wisdom and sanctity of the dead. Voltaire had genius, imagination, feeling, and poetry, and these gifts always have been, and always will be, incompatible with the practice of law. While he was studying law, he was writing verses: verses that were wicked, sacrilegious, and sometimes malicious. He was also making up for the play he missed in youth and was having a gay time with his friends. On account of some boyish scrape, he was sent by his father to Caen and, although in a way under restraint, at once captured the society and intellect of the town. His father, seeing something of the boy's brilliancy, sent him word that if he would come back home he would buy him a good post in the government. "Tell my father," was the answer, "I do not want any place that can be bought. I will make one for myself that will cost nothing." Later in his life, in writing the story of the great dramatist Molière, he said, "All who have made a name for themselves in the fine arts, have done so in spite of their relations. Nature has always been much stronger with them than education," and again, "I saw early that one can neither resist one's ruling passion nor fight one's destiny."

Voltaire is only one illustration of the wisdom of these remarks. The usual is always mediocre. When nature takes it into her head to make a man, she fits him with her own equipment and educates him in her own school.

His father got him a post in Holland, where he wrote more verses, and fell in love, or at least thought he did, which comes to the same thing. He was forbidden to see his mistress. After various difficulties in meeting, she wisely concluded that the chances were so uncertain she had better take someone else. Naturally this serious matter made a deep impression on a boy. He concluded there was nothing to live for and turned more deliberately to literature for consolation. He went seriously to work and never stopped until he died at eighty-four. Had he been able to marry the girl, then—but what's the use in speculating upon that?

Louis XIV died in 1715. His reign was splendid, corrupt and profligate. The people were hungry and turbulent; the notables tyrannical and insolent. The last few years the king was the absolute monarch of France, and he was ruled by a woman and a priest. The news of his death was received with joy by the multitude. Young Voltaire was at the funeral. This funeral resembled a fête more than a day of mourning.

Voltaire by this time was known for his epigrams, his rhymes and his audacity. The salons of Paris were at once opened to him. Whatever else he was during his life, he was never dull, and the world forgives almost anything but stupidity. Commencing early in his life, most of the epigrams and brilliant satires in France were charged to Voltaire. On account of a particularly odious epigram, he was exiled to Sully. His keepers found him a most agreeable guest, and he was at once a favorite in the society of the place. "It would be delightful to stay at Sully," he wrote, "if I were only allowed to go away from it." He spent his time hunting, flirting and writing verses. In his verses and his epigrams he could flatter when he thought flattery would accomplish his end, and by this means his exile was brought to a close and he returned to Paris after an absence of about a year.

No sooner was he back, than a violent attack on the government appeared. This was at once charged to Voltaire, who had in fact not written it. During this time he had been writing his first play, which had been accepted and was then on rehearsal at the theater, but on account of the anonymous verses, which he did not write, he was sent to the Bastille. A few days after he was placed in prison he signed a receipt for "two volumes of Homer, two Indian kerchiefs, a little cap, two cravats, a night cap and a bottle of essence of cloves."

It was some time before he was given a pen and ink, which all his life he needed more than anything else; but without these, he began to compose a new play. He was able to carry in his mind whole cantos of the play and, as Frederick the Great said, "His prison became his Parnassus." Voltaire was not the first or last man to convert a prison into a hall of fame. A prison is confining to the body, but whether it affects the mind, depends entirely upon the mind.

It was while in prison that he changed his named from the one his father gave him—Arouet—to the one he has made famous throughout all time—Voltaire. He said, "I was very unlucky under my first name. I want to see if this one will succeed any better."

His verses soon won him the clemency of the regent, who wrote him, "Be prudent and I will provide for you." Voltaire answered, "I shall be delighted if your highness will give me my board but beg that you will take no further trouble about my lodging." In a year he was released, but whether in prison or surrounded by the gayest court in Europe, he was always forging his keen, witty, malicious darts against the enemies of truth and liberty.

When Voltaire was twenty-four, his first play, *Oedipe,* was produced in Paris. His verses and epigrams had already made him famous throughout the capital and a packed house made up of the intellectual and important people of Paris greeted the play with wild enthusiasm. It ran for forty-five nights, and at once made Voltaire famous as a playwright; which fame was with him to the end. This play, together with his earlier works, got him a pension, but the pension did not succeed in keeping his mouth closed, as is generally the case. Pensions are the favors of the powerful, and dangerous to any great intellect. It is only here and there down throughout the ages that a Voltaire is born who does not fall a victim to their blandishments. Not only pensions, but what the world calls good society, was always open to Voltaire. He needed but to obey the mandates of the rules to live as the pampered child of luxury and ease, but this Voltaire always refused to do. He went his way writing his plays, making his epigrams, reading his verses, witty, audacious and heterodox, dodging officers and jails, doing his own work, flattering those whom he despised, managed to keep out of jail most of the time, and died at the old age of eighty-four.

Much of his work he did while confined to his bed. He was always an invalid, always obliged to take great care of himself, living constantly with death just before him, never idle a moment for fear his work would not be done. Probably no man ever lived who assailed the Church and the State with the same wit and keenness that was always at Voltaire's command; and yet in spite of this he managed to live comfortably, accumulate riches and die in peace.

Voltaire with all his other talents was a businessman. For

this he has been criticized by biographers and enemies. While he was ever generous to his friends and ready to give his time and money for an unpopular cause, he constantly haggled and dickered over business matters and seldom got the worst of any trade. No iconoclast can possibly escape the severest criticism. If he is poor he is against existing things because he cannot succeed. If he is rich, he is not faithful to his ideals. The world always demands of a prophet a double standard. He must live a life consistent with his dreams, and at the same time must obey the conventions of the world. He cannot be judged either by one or the other, but must be judged by both. In trying to live up to both standards, one invariably misses both. It is hard to be true to the two, especially when the standards of the new and the old are in conflict. The ravens should feed the iconoclasts, but they don't.

Voltaire loved the good things of life. He loved society; he loved the witty and intelligent; he loved fame; and he was singularly vain. He loved the society of the courts of Europe. He spent many days at the magnificent courts of France, adapting himself the best he could, but at the same time seeing through its shams, despising its vanities, its cruelties and its injustice to the poor; but he must do his work, and to do his work in France two hundred years ago, he must have the patronage of princes, of priest, of kings and influential courtesans.

Writing from the court of Louis XV, he says, "It is a dreadful bore to be here, but it is very advantageous—the cage is so exquisitely gilded that one must try not to see the bars through the gold." For another of his brilliant sayings he was thrown into the Bastille for a short time in 1726. He was pardoned on the condition that he go to England. No sooner had he reached that island than he was at once received by the poets, philosophers and statesmen of England.

Swift, Pope, Young, Gray and Walpole were then shedding their luster on the British isle. Newton was dying and Locke, though dead, had just begun to speak.

Voltaire at once threw himself into the life of England. Here he found a land where one could write and speak and publish his honest thoughts. Here he felt that he had reached the "promised land." He was everywhere received by the intellectual spirits of England, and within six months he was master of the English tongue, and all the rest of his life could read and speak that language almost as fluently as if native born. Here he met the Quakers, studied their religion, and was captivated by their simplicity and their tolerance. "What! you have no priests?" said Voltaire to the Quaker. "No, friend," he replied, "and we get along very well without them."

Voltaire was an admirer of the English and their land. He found "greatness without insolence and without Bastilles." "It has taken seas of blood to drown the idol of despotism, but the English do not think they bought their laws too dearly." When he was an old man he said he once lived in a land "where a professor of mathematics, only because he was great in his vocation, had been buried like a king who had done good to his subjects." He spoke of Locke as the "wisest of human beings." "The catechism reveals God to children, but Newton has revealed him to sages." "Locke dared sometimes to speak positively, but he also dared to doubt." "I love people who say what they think. We only half live if we dare only half think." "What would you have done had you been born in Spain?" asked Voltaire's secretary. "I would have gone to mass every day, kissed the monk's robes and set fire to their convents."

Voltaire's residence in England made a great impression on his future life. He seemed to dedicate himself anew to the great cause of human liberty. He felt that it was for him to destroy oppression, superstition and tyranny. He never ceased to fight for the cause as long as life remained.

After three years in England, Voltaire managed to get permission to return to Paris. He set to work to write another play and to organize a company to act it. During all his life he was passionately fond of the stage, writing plays on every subject, ancient and modern, plays which always held keen thrusts against the injustice of the world. He was busy organizing companies to produce his plays, constantly associated with actors; in his later years he built a theater of his own at Ferney and frequently took part on the stage in his own plays. In those days the business of an actor was more despised than it is today. Actors were servants of the rich, men and women who contributed to their pleasure for the purpose of satisfying their idle hours. Everybody went to the theater, but no one had any regard for those who performed a part. While the king might sit in a box, the dead player could not be buried in consecrated ground.

Soon after his return to Paris, Adrienne Lecouvreur died at the age of thirty-eight. She was the greatest actress of her time and her death made a profound impression upon Voltaire. He had known her in her younger years; had been her friend and admirer up to the time of her death. She was a woman of genius and intellect. She was taken with a fatal illness while playing one of Voltaire's plays. Voltaire hastened to her bedside. She died in his arms, in agony for which the doctors of that day could furnish no relief. Her fame and her fate made a profound impression in Paris at the time.

In her death she could have neither priest nor absolution; was denied Christian burial; taken out of the city at night and "thrown in the kennel" like a dog. It was said of this brilliant woman that "she had all the virtues but virtue." Whatever she was, her life had been no worse than the paramours, friends and mistresses of the kings and nobles over whose graves priests had pronounced eulogies and benedictions, and who had been laid in consecrated ground; but her intellect, her genius, and her heart were far above all these. For a time Voltaire forgot to be a cynic, but was touched to the soul by the injustice of the French law, French society and French religion. He had been, he said, "her admirer, her friend, and her lover." "Shall I ever cease to see," he wrote, "the light-minded Frenchman sleeping under the rule of superstitition?" Is it only in England that mortals dare to think? Men deprived of burial here to whom Greece would have raised altars! In London she would have had a tomb among geniuses, kings and heroes. Ye gods, why is my country no longer the fatherland of glory and talent?"

During the rest of his he worked tirelessly to improve the condition of the actors of his day. Even as an old man he could never forget the injustice done to this great woman. "Actors are paid by the king," he said, "and excommunicated by the church. They are commanded by the king to play every evening and by the church forbidden to do so at all. If they do not play, they are put in prison. If they do, they are spurned into a kennel. We delight to live with them and object to be buried with them. We admit them to our tables and exclude them from our cemeteries." Even in old age, singularly enough, his greatest dread was that he might be thrown in the gutter after his death.

There was no field of literature that was not open to Voltaire. A poet, an essayist, a writer of plays, a historian, a novelist, a scientist, a philosopher. He tried them all and excelled in all. His histories were as brilliant as his plays. He understood, as well as any man who ever lived, the difficulty that besets the author who would write history. "Whoso writes a history of his own times," he says, "must be expected to be blamed for everything he has said and everything he has not said."

His *English Letters* had been prepared in England and after his return to France. These, he knew, were too dangerous to be published in Paris. He was saving them until it might be safe. Somehow they were stolen and appeared in 1734. These letters contained studies of the great English philosophers and comments on life, which were modern then and are still modern. The truth is always modern and there never comes a time when it is safe to give it voice.

The publisher of his *English Letters* was thrown into the Bastille, the book was denounced and publicly burned in Paris by the hangman as "scandalously contrary to religion, morals and society," but still Paris was not so old-fashioned. Men are constantly thrown into prison today in America for publications which are "scandalous" and "contrary to morals and authority"—publications which tell the truth, and which are condemned simply because they tell the truth. Voltaire's house was searched, but he got the news in time and once more fled to save his liberty and his life.

There is no parallel in history for this great genius. Born in Paris, placed in the Bastille for audacious writing at eighteen, driven to Holland, to England, Prussia and the far-off provinces of France. All his life he loved Paris, and although he died at an advanced age, probably five or six years would cover all the time that he lived in Paris during his mature life.

Voltaire could not keep out of trouble. Almost every person of importance was his enemy at some period of his life, but he was not a nonresistant. He never turned the other cheek. When he was attacked, he replied with pamphlets and epigrams more poisonous than those any other author ever penned. Whenever he was at peace, he was uneasy to be at war. If his critics and traducers let him alone for a time, he was busy writing some pamphlet, poem or play to get himself into trouble once more. He seldom signed his own name to the production of his pen. More than one hundred names were used by Voltaire in the course of his long literary career, but whatever the name and whether written by him or not, if especially bitter, mocking, rebellious or ungodly, it was always laid to Voltaire; and whatever the utterance that made the trouble, whether it was his or not, Voltaire was ready to deny that he was the author.

Most of his pamphlets and many of his more pretentious works he promptly denied. He did not write the pamphlet or the poem. He did not write the essay on Natural Rights. He did not write the attack on priest or king. He did not write the *Philosophical Dictionary*. He had nothing to do with the *Encyclopedia*. He wrote only words of flattery for the king and nicely turned stanzas for the women of the court. He sometimes condemned his own books and was present in the crowd to see them burned, but no doubt most men would have preferred to deny the pamphlets than to have been burned with them. It is idle to speculate whether a man should or should not have done this or that. No doubt some men would have been burned with the first pamphlet that they wrote, but not Voltaire. He preferred to live to an old age and dodge and flee and deny and lie and still pour forth upon the world the greatest mass of rebellious literature that ever came from the pen of man.

Voltaire fled from Paris when the *English Letters* were published. He fled to a distant part of France. From there he went to live on an old estate with Madame du Chatelet and her husband. The husband was an army officer and seldom at home, and of very little consequence when he was. Madame du Chatelet was one of the most remarkable women of her age, or any other. Brilliant and learned, she loved pleasure and she loved work. No book was too deep for her understanding. She was a mathematician, an astronomer, a philosopher and a woman. Voltaire was forty years of age when he fled from Paris to the estate of Madame du Chatelet and his life and fortunes were bound up with her for sixteen years. The estate was old and dilapidated and in a barren and dreary part of France, but with his industry and his money, he made it a place of beauty sought by the greatest people of Europe.

Madame du Chatelet was not a housekeeper. She never swept the floor or dusted books or knew how to cook a meal or to see that anyone else did it. She was intellectual, and no woman ought to expect to be intellectual and a housekeeper too. She was difficult, irascible, and voluble. Voltaire was impressionable, sensitive, quick-tempered. They kept each other very much entertained. Sometimes they loved, often they fought, but still they seemed to find each other necessary for their work. Together they studied astronomy, mathematics, philosophy, history and religion. Together they visited nobles, princes and courts, perhaps "the most brilliant pair in France" of that day. No doubt after some years, the tie between them grew galling to Voltaire, and perhaps to Madame du Chatelet, but it had grown to be a habit. Had they been married, they would probably have gotten a divorce; but as they were not married, they could not be divorced and stayed together.

Voltaire was particularly blessed by two women, Madame du Chatelet, at whose estate he lived for sixteen years, and Madame Denis, his niece, who kept his house near Geneva for more than twenty-five years. Neither of them gave him a moment's peace, and forced him to flee to his study for consolation and rest. If either of these women had made his life comfortable his great work would probably never have been done.

There are two things that kill a genius—a fatal disease and contentment. When a man is contented he goes to sleep. Voltaire had no chance to be contented, and so he wrote eternally and unceasingly, more than any other man in the history of the world. Toward the end, the relations of these two grew galling in the extreme, until finally Madame du Chatelet transferred her affections to a young army officer who lived in the house, a protégé and friend of Voltaire. Soon after she died and Voltaire was without a home.

While Voltaire was living with Madame du Chatelet in the far province, he was always yearning for Paris. Scheming, conniving, urging his friends to get him the right to return. "I will declare that all priests are disinterested; that the Jesuits are honest; that the inquisition is the triumph of humanity and tolerance. In face I will say anything they like if they will but leave me in peace."

During this time there was growing up that deep and weird friendship with Frederick the Great. Frederick was then a prince, but would one day be king of Prussia. He was skeptical, tolerant and filled with humane thoughts. He hated war, he loved learning, he appreciated Voltaire and, with his keen insight, set him down as the greatest man in Europe. The letters between the two were voluminous and continued through all sorts of difficulties and quarrels to the time of his death. Frederick addressed him as "dearest friend," "charming, divine, Voltaire," "sublime spirit," "first of thinking beings." To Voltaire Frederick was "Marcus Aurelius," "the star of the North," "not a king among kings, but a king among men." Frederick replied that his "whole creed was one God and one Voltaire." For a long time they worshiped each other at a distance, which is always a safe way to worship. Frederick constantly urged Voltaire to come to his court, but Madame du Chatelet was in the way. She was extremely jealous. For a long time she kept him from making the journey, Frederick urged him to come, so he arranged to take Madame du Chatelet with him. Frederick replied that he could bring her if he wished, but he preferred to have him come alone. Finally, with great reluctance, Madame du Chatelet granted him a leave of absence and he made the journey.

The king and Voltaire were fascinated with each other for a time. Voltaire corrected Frederick's verses, helped him about his French, entertained him and his brilliant company, swapped compliments with him, and was the life of his court; but all geniuses are difficult, especially when more than one is present at the same time. Genius cannot be confined to narrow limits or to fixed conventions even though they are the limits and conventions of another genius. Their friendship grew strained and Voltaire went away, went back to Madame du Chatelet; but still they continued to write. With the long distance between them, Voltaire was the greatest man that ever lived and Frederick the greatest prince on earth. Both Frederick and Voltaire hated war. Both of them believed that there was something better for men than to kill each other. Voltaire looked for great things from Frederick when he should become king.

About the first act of his reign was to declare war. Somehow the king's business looked different to him when he was the king. Voltaire could not understand it. He was shocked and grieved and wrote and pleaded with Frederick to abandon war and follow his instincts for peace; to build up a great kingdom dedicated to liberty, to humanity, to justice for all.

Voltaire made no concealment of his disappointment with Frederick's acts and his changed views, but still they were friends. Through many years they wrote constantly to each. other, letters on philosophy, literature, religion, life, morals and war; but still Voltraire stayed on at Madame du Chatelet's estate.

When Voltaire was fifty years old, Cardinal Fleury died. He was a member of the French Academy and Voltaire wanted his place. What the membership could do for Voltaire, is hard to understand, but no one likes bubbles and trinkets and decorations as do the great. Voltaire set himself to work to get this place. Madame du Chatelet helped. He must have the king and to get the king he must have his favorite mistress, who at that time was Madame du Pompadour, but neither could do anything without the pope. So Voltaire set to work, first, on Madame du Pompadour. He wrote her verses. One of the poems begins:

Every grace and charm and art,
Pompadour, in you is found.

Of course she "fell for it." She got the king on his side. Then he started for the pope. Voltaire never did anything halfway. If he wanted a thing he went after it. He was always afraid of doing too little, but never afraid he was doing too much.

He had already written his play *Mahomet*. This of course had been pronounced sacrilegious and profane and had been consiged to the flames. Still he thought the pople did not fully understand the play. He wrote long letters to people in society to prove what a good Christian and church man he was, but he did not succeed in deceiving anyone. The Academy could not accept him as a successor to a cardinal, but England elected him a member of the Royal Society. Germany placed him in her Hall of Fame. Everybody recognized him but France. Still he was not satisfied. Then he started a still bolder campaign to mollify the pope. He read all his works, complimented him highly and thereupon the pope called him his "dear son" and sent Voltaire his "blessing." Then he wrote the pope asking permission to dedicate to him his play *Mahomet*, and although it had been burned as sacrilegious, the pope consented. The pope doubtless thought it would be better to have Voltaire his friend than his enemy, so he sent Voltaire his "apostolic benediction" and accepted the dedication of "your admirable tragedy." Voltaire replied that he "laid the work against the founder of a false religion, at the feet of the chief of the true religion." He flattered the cardinals and went into ecstasy over the pope's virtues.

With Madame Pompadour, the king and the pope at his back, he could not fail. Another vacancy occurred a few years later and Voltaire, at the age of fifty-two, was admitted to the French Academy, long after he had been admitted to almost every other great society in Europe.

It was the custom of the new members to read a paper, so Voltaire read one to the Academy. At once he became Voltaire. The paper was witty, audacious and sacrilegious. It offended all the august personages who heard and read it. They regretted that he was a member of the Academy, but it was too late. They should have known before that such a leopard could not change its spots. Again he was chased from the court. Again he went to Madame du Chatelet.

When Madame du Chatelet was really dead, Voltaire was overwhelmed with grief. During all their years together, Voltaire had held her in unbounded admiration. Thirteen years before her death, he had given her his portrait engraved with these lines:

Bavier 'graved this likeness for you,
Recognize it and his art.
As for me, a greater master
Has engraved you on my heart.

The death of Madame du Chatelet sent him adrift in the world.

He had enemies and spiteful critics throughout France. "To sit high is to be lied about."

Frederick the Great saw his opportunity. He still loved Voltaire. He loved him with an affection that although often rent and clouded by doubts and discord, remained with him to his death. He besought Voltaire to come to Berlin. He offered him honors and a pension, decorations and the society of the wise and great. Voltaire, with no one to deny him, could not resist and went. He reached Berlin in the midst of a great public fête. The populace forgot the king and worshiped Voltaire. The king took him to his palace at Potsdam, fitted him a suite of rooms in royal state and made him his constant companion. All of the king's literary productions he turned over to Voltaire for correction and revision, and after they left Voltaire's hands, they did honor to any prince. But it is not wise for even the closest affinities to be kept constantly together, especially if these affinities are brilliant.

Again a coldness arose between Voltaire and Frederick. In the meantime Voltaire entered into a business speculation which resulted in a lawsuit, bringing scandal on the court. The breach between them widened until they could no longer stay together. After about three years, Voltaire precipitately fled from Berlin. He fled because he feared arrest. He made his way with all haste to the German frontier, but before he crossed the line, the agents of the king placed him under arrest. He was detained several days, mainly to get from him the manuscript which Frederick had written while a prince and which severely attacked the Christian religion. It was all right while he was a prince, but would not do after he became a king. Still the world is not so much changed, and even Mark Twain in his later days wrote a vigorous attack on Christianity, which he printed for private circulation alone.

Voltaire was soon permitted to go on his way, but he felt humiliated and outraged by the man who had been his friend. Voltaire never saw Frederick the Great after his flight, but they still had the old yearning for each other. Letters were exchanged almost as frequently as before and Frederick the Great paid him one of the noblest tributes at his death. The three years he lived at Berlin produced less than any other part of Voltaire's active years. Too much gaiety, too much society, too much admiration, too many quarrels. The genius was for a time reduced to the man. Voltaire himself felt that he had practically wasted the years. He appreciated its tragedy and likewise its comedy. He could laugh at either tragedy or comedy. All his life he could joke and with him there was no subject too serious for a comedy. Voltaire said, "It is because one can be frivolous that the majority of people do not hang themselves." He has often been criticized because he could joke. The ordinary mind cannot understand that a serious purpose and a sense of humor can go together. It is only the sense of humor that can keep a man alive for the serious purpose. The world has never been able to distinguish between stupidity and seriousness. If the stupidly serious really had any humor, they would die from laughing at themselves.

Voltaire spent a short time traveling through various parts of France, fearing to go back to Paris, and then turned to Geneva. Geneva was then an independent state, afterward annexed to France and later to Switzerland. His flight from Prussia and refuge in Geneva marked a new era in his life. He was sixty years old when he reached this little state. He had been sobered by age and experience. He had learned much of the follies and frivolities of the world. He knew that after all, his was a serious life and his work the greatest ever undertaken by man in any age. He seemed to take new vows to the service of the great cause which was really the greatest of his life, the cause of liberty. From that time on, he was tireless, unremitting, and brilliant in that cause. Wherever he found superstition, unjustice, tyranny, and cruelty, Voltaire placed himself in the arena ready for the fray. Whether his work was history, poetry, drama, novels or pamphlets, it was the same. Probably all his works will never be brought together. His pamphlets were numberless and these pamphlets, more than his more pretentious works, influenced France and his age, and through them destroyed old institutions and customs and barbarities, and prepared the world for the toleration and liberty that will some day come.

When Voltaire went to Geneva, that state was still held in the mental paralysis of the doctrines of John Calvin. It was two hundred years since Calvin had piously burned Michael Servitus for the crime of thinking in place of believing. While Calvin had been dead almost as long, the spell of his genius and fanaticism still held the land. Geneva was obsessed by a strange idea—an idea as common now as then—a belief that in spite of civilization, science, philosophy and experience, will not die: the doctrine that men can be changed and made perfect by human laws. The Geneva laws fixed the time at which people should go to bed and get up in the morning, and of course both hours were early; fixed the kind of drink and food and the amount and quality that was proper for a man to take. It regulated the religious creeds and social customs. No matter what one wished to do, he could find out whether it was right or wrong by consulting the statutes of Geneva.

The same obsession rules the human race today. We have changed the diet, the religious, and moral code, the social code, the social customs, but not the fundamental idea that the state should tell us what to do and especially what not to do, and that to disobey is to be a criminal, punished, outlawed, and reviled. Today when the statutes are not sufficiently severe to satisfy the mob, "Mother Grundy" takes up the work and reviles and persecutes and maligns with all the brutality, insolence, cruelty, and ferocity that marked the inquisitors of the ancient world. Of course, theaters and playacting were wrong in Geneva when Voltaire fled from the court of Frederick the Great, but there were two things that Voltaire always determined to do. He was bound to fight hypocrisies and shams and the cruelties of the world, and he was bound to live.

He soon purchased two estates about three miles from Geneva, in the territory of France. He was near enough to Geneva so he could build a theater of his own and the people could come across the border to see his plays and the barbarous laws of Calvin could not forbid. He was near enough to the French border so he could flee to Switzerland or Geneva whenever the king of France should determine to send him to the Bastille. The estate where he spent the great portion of his remaining life, he called Ferney, almost on the shores of the beautiful Lake Geneva, with Mont Blanc and the other Alpine peaks in full view, the clear sky and the snow-capped mountains almost above him, and the green fields of France and Switzerland around him—an ideal spot in which to live and work and dream. It was not for its beauty that he chose this spot. The love of natural beauty never entered the soul of Voltaire. He knew or cared little for art and nothing for nature. Had he lived today, the spacious, elaborate steam-heated flat would have been his idea of a home. Voltaire traveled all over Europe, but never halted to see a beautiful picture, classical statue, grand cathedral, or any scene of great natural beauty or sublimity.

These estates were old and dilapidated and Voltaire set to work to improve them. He commenced cultivating the soil, planting trees, building a house. He hired gardeners, farmers and servants without end. He seemed to know how to turn his mind to agriculture, as well as to writing plays and pamphlets. Like most other philosophers, poets and dreamers, he at least said that he thought agriculture was the one thing worthwhile. Probably like others, he did not mean it. "I have only done one sensible thing in my life," said Voltaire, "to cultivate the ground. He who tills a field, renders a better service to mankind than all the scribblers in Europe."

"You have done a great work for posterity," said a friend one day. "Yes, Madame, I have planted four thousand feet of trees in my park." While many literary men have been farmers, very few of them have made it pay, but Voltaire made it pay. Had he been more religious and less versatile, he could have been the Pierpont Morgan of his age.

Later at Ferney he developed other industries. He imported the silkworm and manufactured silk. He had a large watch factory and the town becaqme a prosperous industrial place. The colony was well paid and satisfied. Workmen sought jobs from all parts of the land, as refugees fled to him for shelter. But still neither farming nor manufacturing was his real work. His pen was never idle.

For years he had been working on a dramatic poem,

Pucelle. It had been read in all the societies of Europe, but never published. It was wicked and ungodly. Women read it in the boudoirs, but not in the parlors. Men kept the copy out of their library, but had it in their private collection. The book was an open secret throughout Europe. Voltaire had always used every means to keep it from the publisher, but his manuscripts were constantly disappearing. His friends and private secretaries were stealing them and selling them. Most authors have hard work to find publishers. Voltaire had hard work to keep publishers from printing his books. One day a publisher called on Voltaire and ofered to sell him a copy of his own book, *Pucelle.* He at once said he did not write it; that it must have been the work of some person who had neither poetic art, good sense, or good morals. He denounced the publisher to the Geneva authorities; but it had escaped the printer in Paris, where everyone was reading it. The authorities burned it and a Parisian publisher was sentenced to nine years at the galleys for printing an edition. Geneva pretended to believe Voltaire's statement that he was not its author and Geneva burned it too. At the same time, Paris was going mad over his other plays, which were attracting crowds at the theaters. The work was everywhere received with applause, but the author was condemned to exile.

On November 1, 1755, Lisbon was destroyed by an earthquake. The news reached Voltaire and stirred him to the soul. Thirty thousand people were destroyed almost in the twinkling of an eye. The earthquake was on All Saints day and the greatest loss of life was in the cathedrals and churches of the place. For months, all his letters contained allusions to this catastrophe, which took possession of his mind. "The best of all possible worlds! If Pope had been there, would he have said, 'Whatever is is right?' 'All is well,' seems to me absurd, when evil is on land and sea."

Voltaire wrote a searching poem on the problems of life, entitled "The Disaster of Lisbon." At the same time was published his poem on "Natural Law" covering the eternal questions as to the meaning, plan, scheme, and end of all. Voltaire answered these questions as all other thinkers have ever answered them, that upon these subjects man has no guide and no light. But the churches and the authorities read, or at least heard of, these two poems. They were promptly burned in Paris and pious Genevans held up their hands in horror at the theology, or rather lack of theology, which they taught. But the Lisbon earthquake shocked the world. Even the king of France had serious thoughts, so serious that he caused the private entrance to Madame Pompadour's apartments to be closed and made her a maid of honor to the queen.

About this time, an unfortunate lunatic named Damins made a weak attempt on the life of Louis XV. The orthodox in church and state said that plainly the act was inspired by the New Thought of that day. It was perfectly easy to trace the act of a crazy man to the writings of Voltaire, which the man had never read. True, when the man was captured, he had in his hand a copy of the New Testament. Voltaire was delighted when he got this news. "A testament? I told you so. All assassins have a Bible with their daggers, but have you ever heard of one who had a Cicero, a Plato, or a Virgil?"

The assault on the king threw politicians and statesmen into panic all over Europe and at once they began to make the penal code more barbarous, the prohibitory laws stricter, and the censorship of the press more complete. There was but one way to deal wtih the act of a crazy man and that was to persecute and torture thousands of innocent ones.

This was two hundred years ago, but every penal code

in the United States has been made more savage and barbarous and the people, if possible, more brutal and unreasoning, because an insane man killed the President of the United States. How the world does change!

During many years Ferney was a Mecca for the great and the learned of the world. Voltaire kept open house. He was bound to be active no matter what he thought or tried to do. He knew that constant activity was the only answer to the meaning of "life." As Voltaire put it, "Tranquility is a beautiful thing, but boredom is of its acquaintance and family."

In his house in Ferney, he installed his niece, Madame Denis, or rather she installed herself. She was uncouth, talkative, and fond of pleasure. She loved to consort with the great, but bored everyone she met. She took possession of his house and life. Much of his company was due to her. Many of his activities were for her amusement and to keep her still; but she at least kept him busy and made him work. A constant stream of visitors poured into Ferney through all these years. He had some sixty servants, besides the other employees of the place, but these were kept busy looking after travelers and friends. No one was denied admission, whether rich or poor, whether priest or pagan. All were housed and fed. When the hotels were closed at Geneva, the people went to Ferney, where they could get board and lodging free. Voltaire said that for fourteen years he was the innkeeper of Europe. Here he built his theater and brought the greatest actors and actresses of the day, played himself, entertained his company and his friends and the constant stream of visitors who came from Geneva to see the plays. Even Madame Denis was kept from boredom by the life of Ferney.

In Geneva lived Jean-Jacques Rousseau. He too was a rebel, mighty in war. Voltaire was keener, wittier, deeper, greater. Rousseau was more fiery, emotional, passionate. Both were really warriors in the same great cause. From their different places, three miles apart, both sent forth their thunderbolts to wake a sleeping world. When the world awakened and shook itself, churches, thrones, institutions, laws, and customs were buried in the wreck. Some charged the wreck to Voltaire, some to Rousseau.

These two men, engaged in the same cause, fighting the same foes, could not agree. Rousseau joined with the clergy of Geneva in defaming Voltaire's theater and his plays. Voltaire fought back with weapons keener than any Rousseau knew how to use. Two geniuses cannot possibly live so close together. In fact, the world itself is hardly big enough for two at the same time. As Wendell Phillips once said: "No one hates a reformer as much as another reformer," and the war of these two men was long and bitter. It ended only with death, when both were brought to Paris and placed in the Pantheon, side by side, where they managed to stay in harmony until a frenzied religious mob sacked their tombs, burned them with quicklime and visited the vengeance upon them when dead which they never could wreak before.

In making his improvements and overhauling the estate at Ferney, Voltaire built a new church. On the estate was one, dilapidated and old, which did not fit the new surroundings, and so long as he was to have a church, he wanted one that would ornament the place. He set to work about this, as he did at everything in life, vigorously and thoroughly. He would have a church that was a church and which would be as orthodox as any in Christendom.

For a long time he had been attending mass regularly every Sunday, taking with him his adopted child and the members of his household and setting a good example to the people on the estate. He would have a church as orthodox

and as regular as Notre Dame, so he put himself in com-
munciation with the pope and asked for a bull granting him
absolute power over his churchyard, and for some sacred
relics for the church. The request was granted and the Holy
Father sent a piece of the hair shirt of St. Francis of Assisi,
the patron saint. On the same day came a present of the
portrait of Madame du Pompadour, and Voltaire remarked,
"So, you see, I am all right both for this world and the next."
He dedicated his church to "God alone" and was fond of
saying that it was the only church in the universe that was
dedicated to "God alone" and not to a saint. "For my part,"
he said, "I would rather build for the Master than for the
servants." Then he designed for him a tomb attached to the
church and jutting out from the wall. "The wicked will say,"
he remarked, "that I am neither inside nor out."

Later he shocked the holy people by going into the pulpit
himself to preach. Not only did he have a church but he
had a priest of his own who had lived with him at his house.
An easygoing, companionable man, who cared for or paid
little attention to religious matters. His name was Adam. For
the most part, Father Adam's duties were to play chess with
Voltaire, and when he wanted him for a game of chess he
would call loudly to him, "Where art thou, Adam?"

He practically forced the priests to listen to his confession
and bestow their benedictions upon him, but while he was
toying with his own church, consorting with the priests, cor-
responding with the pope and attending mass, he was always
forging his thunderbolts against the church.

For the last twenty-five years of his life, the superstition,
the ignorance, and above all, the cruelty of the church, was
constantly in his mind. He scarcely wrote a letter, a tract
or book, that he did not revert to these over and over again,
and in spite of all his contortions and sumersaults, there

probably cannot be found a line of Voltaire which defended superstition, gave countenance to cruelty or barbarism, and did not plead for the enlightenment and freedom of man.

His life at Ferney was one of constant work. All day he was busy with his books, his writings and his farm. The evening he gave up to the pleasures of society and to the *Encyclopedia* which was carried forward by the wisest men of France. Here he wrote volume after volume of his *Philosophical Dictionary,* every page filled with subtle and deadly stabs at the church. Here he poured forth his pamphlets without number, sowing the seeds of revolution and revolt. "What harm can a book do that costs a hundred crowns," wrote Voltaire, "Twenty volumes folio will never make a revolution. It is the little pocket pamphlets of thirty sous that are to be feared." Here too he wrote his letters; letters to all kinds of people, especially scholars and rulers—letters more voluminous than ever came from the pen of any other correspondent in the world. Seven thousand of these have been preserved and printed and no one knows how many more are lost forever. These letters, like his pamphlets and his books, were ever urging tolerance, enlightenment, and the freedom of the mind.

Voltaire hated prisons and hated war. He was a bitter foe, but always quick and generous to forgive. With his servants on his place, he was generous and indulgent in the extreme. On one occasion two of the house servants robbed their master. The police discovered it and were hot on their trail. Voltaire bade his secretary to see the servants and urge them to flee. ":"For if they are arrested," he said, "I shall not be able to save them from hanging." He gave them money for their journey and helped them in every way he could.

His many acts of humanity could not be recorded. His fight for Jean Calas is one of the most heroical of this or any other age. Calas was an old resident of Toulouse. Toulouse, like all the rest of France, was an intensely religious town. The priests and the state religion held full sway. Calas was a Protestant and a respected merchant of the place; all his family were Protestants, except one son, who had joined the Catholic Church. Another son, who like his father was a Protestant, decided to study law, but he could not be admitted to practice unless he joined the established church. He grew despondent and morose and hanged himself. He was discovered in a room of the house, dead, and hanging by the neck. His family and friends sought to conceal the act, as suicide in those days, as now, was a mortal crime. One should have nothing to say either about coming into the world or going out. A suicide's soul would go to hell, but at that time his body would be drawn and quartered and thrown to the dogs. Someone of the people, which means the mob, started the cry that the son was about to become a Catholic and the father had murdered him. This was taken up until the whole city was worked to a frenzy against the helpless old man and his family. The body of the dead was taken from the home and buried in state from the cathedral with all the rites and ceremonies of the Catholic Church. Calas was arrested, tried, and of course condemned. He was old and feeble and could not have committed the deed even had there been any motive or desire. Of course there was no substantial evidence. Someone testified that a neighbor had told them that another neighbor had said that a peddler had seen Calas coming from the room where the son was hanged. Of course the peddler was not found, neither the one to whom he had talked.

In those days, hearsay evidence was a favorite kind. In two hundred years we have banished hearsay evidence from the courts of justice, and today it finds favor only with Madam

Grundy, the strongest monarch in the world. Calas was doomed to torture and to death. His wrists were bound to an iron ring fastened to a stone post; his feet to another ring in the floor. They then turned the wheel until every joint in his arms and legs was dislocated. He was brought back to life, asked to confess, but he still refused. They contrived further tortures which still failed to bring a confession. The executioner then bound him to a wooden cross, broke his legs and arms with an iron bar and strangled him. Then they took his body, chained it to a stake and he was burned. His property was confiscated, his sons and daughters placed in Catholic institutions and the widow left to wander where she would.

This revolting affair was brought to the attention of Voltaire at Ferney. Calas was dead, but the system still lived. He took one of the sons into his home, learned the facts, corresponded with all the notable people of Europe, industriously prepared the case, hired a lawyer and presented the case for review to the parliament of Paris. In this case he enlisted Frederick the Great, Catherine of Russia, and many other illustrious people throughout Europe. For six years his interest never flagged. Calas had been condemned by all the judges, excepting one. This man, though a churchman like the rest, would not consent. He joined with Voltaire to annul the findings of the court. After six years of constant battle, the parliament of Paris, by unanimous opinion, decided that Calas was innocent of any crime. The estate was given back to the family and the children to their mother. Voltaire raised a large amount of money to take care of the family during the trial and to give them an estate after the vindication was complete.

No sooner was this case disposed of, than another equally horrible appealed to him for help. A boy nineteen years old named LaBare was charged, with several other boys, with having torn down a sacred crucifix. There was no evidence that he committed the heinous offense, but he did confess that he had sung some irreligious songs. LaBare was a reader of Voltaire's *Philosophical Dictionary*; also of the great Diderot. This was enough. He was condemned to death. His tongue was pulled out with hot irons, his head cut off, his body thrown into the flames, together with the *Philosophical Dictionary,* which inspired the horrible deed. In the meantime, his companions had fled to Voltaire. Voltaire took up the case, had the judgment reversed, LaBare's comrades saved and the name of the dead boy cleared of the "terrible" crime.

Many other cases almost as revolting were brought to Voltaire's attention and received his help. Of course in these cases the victim was dead, and it was easier to clear a dead victim than a live one. The most barbarous and ferocious of men and women begin to think and feel remorseful when the deed is done.

But the great battle of Voltaire for the memory of those tortured dead no doubt saved many other innocent men from the same cruel fate and went a long way toward ridding the world of the cruelty and barbarism of his age.

Voltaire no doubt realized that his long years of work were probably responsible for the charges of heresy lodged against many of the victims. They had believed what Voltaire had taught. He had written his *Philosophical Dictionary* full of mockery and profundity; it was audacious in the extreme and a deadly attack upon the superstition of his time. Surreptitiously he had brought it to Geneva and then denied its authorship. "If there is the least danger about it," said Voltaire, "please warn me and then I can disown it in all the public papers with my usual candor and innocence."

The world today, in court and out, acts upon the same

reasoning as the judges in France at the time of Voltaire. Those who speak are often held responsible, in court and out, for the revolutionary acts of men whom they never saw or of whom they never heard. It is cruel to charge men criminally with the result of their words and thoughts. No doubt there is much immature talking and hasty writing and will always be where liberty of speech and press prevails. The political, religious, and social views of any age and even of the most radical members of society, were born, long before their time. Those who invented the alphabet and the printing press are indirectly responsible for much of the violence of a changing social state; but in the same way, they are responsible for the progress of the world, for the enlightenment, for the civilization, and for all that makes the present better than the past. Great changes never did and never can come unless accompanied by violence, by cruelty, by suffering and by pain. These are incident to the progress of the race; they are the labor pains that herald the birth of a new civilization and a better social life.

As Voltaire grew older, life flowed on with an easier current at Ferney. In this prosperous and industrious town, the Huguenot and the Catholic, infidel and believer, worked and lived together in harmony and peace. He developed liberty and tolerance at home and all around him. He had there the practical realization of what was his dream for the human race.

All his life he was a child filled with sports and fancies, mixing with all the pleasures of the young. Ferney was crowded with a pleasure-loving, joyous throng. With all his other activities, he was a great matchmaker. He said himself that he had brought about more than forty marriages, but he never made a match for himself. All his life he was canny and sly.

He was urged by the Russian ruler to write a history of what Frederick the Great called "that barbarous land," but he early saw the possibility of that vast unexplored nation and the Russian force and genius that was behind it all. Catherine of Russia was one of his friends. She was philosophical, skeptical, industrious, cruel and cold, but she was awake to all the modern thought of the world. She believed in the philosophy of Voltaire and in the main used her genius to develop the future greatness of that new land. Catherine the Great was supposed to have killed her husband who was a weakling, that she might rule in his stead. Some of Voltaire's admirers objected to his intimacy with a woman of that type. "O," he said, "that bagatelle about a husband. Those are family affairs with which I do not mix myself."

Voltaire clearly saw the effects of the new intellectual life that was coming to the world. He knew what his years of toil would mean to France. The unnumbered pamphlets that had fallen over the land for sixty years, thick as the winter snow that falls from the clouds, he was certain would bear fruit. Not only what he had done, but what had been done by Rousseau and Diderot and the other writers and thinkers of his age, was bound at last permanently to affect the world. Then, too, the earth had grown tired of kings and princes who lived upon the unpaid labor of the poor. It had grown tired of the priests and superstitions which covered the land with a pall of night. France was awakening. The day was dawning.

Only a few years before the thunderbolt of the French revolution burst with fire and sword upon the earth, he wrote: "Everything I see shows the signs of a revolution which must infallibly come. I shall not have the pleasure of beholding it. The French reach everything late, but they do reach it at last. Young people are lucky. They will see great things.

I shall not cease to preach tolerance upon the housetops until persecution is no more. The progress of the right is slow. The roots of prejudice deep. I shall never see the fruits of my efforts, but their seeds must one day germinate."

At Ferney, at the age of eighty-three, Voltaire wrote his last play, *Irene.* This play was to be produced in the National Theater at Paris. With this thought strongly in mind, a longing to see Paris once more began to overwhelm him. Madam Denis was anxious to go back; although she was growing old she yet longed for the chatter of the crowd. She urged Voltaire to go. All his friends urged him to go. "Paris," said Voltaire, "do you not know that there are forty thousand fanatics who would being forty thousand fagots to burn me? That would be my bed of honor."

Louis XVI was then on the throne. He had most of the faults of the old king, but with these faults he was little short of an imbecile. He hated Voltaire. He knew what the works of Voltaire and Rousseau meant to the world. "These two men have lost France," said the king. Still, he wanted to go. He would like to put *Irene* on the stage himself, to be present at its rehearsal, to see to every detail of its production; so in February 1778, he set out for Paris. The people of his little colony were heartbroken at his departure. Although he said he would return in six weeks, at the latest, they never expected to see his face again. His journey to Paris took five days. It was a royal procession that greeted the old men all the way from Ferney to the capital. Men, women, and children turned out at every town to do him honor. This man who had been in prison, repeatedly exiled and forbidden his city, was returning after twenty-eight years to the home of his birth.

He was the intellectual king of France, if not of the world. Morley calls Voltaire's last visit to Paris one of the "historic events of the century." The philosophers, dramatists, members of the Academy, and above all, the people stood around in crowds to worship at his shrine. Nobles and churchmen stood by sullen, insolent and ominous. He was denounced from the pulpit and called "Anti-Christ"; gladly would they have sent him once more to the Bastille, but they did not dare. Full well they knew that it needed but a match to start a conflagration which would forever destroy the old regime. His rooms at the Hotel Villette were crowded with the intellectuals of the capital day after day. Here came Dr. Franklin presenting his grandson, a boy of seventeen. Voltaire raised his hand above the boy's head and blessed him with the words "God" and "Liberty." Literary men, actors, ambassadors were to do him honor. Madame Du Barry came from her place of banishment to see the intellectual king. Madame du Pompadour had grown old, and died, and Madame Du Barry had taken her place as the favorite courtesan, the most powerful of the women who ruled the court; but on the approach of the revolution she was banished to appease the crowd. All this was too much for old Voltaire. He fell ill and his friends feared for his life. The priest came to get a confession from Voltaire. His confession would be fame enough for any priest.

On February twenty-eighth, when he believed his last hour had come, in the presence of his secretary he wrote down his Confession of Faith: "I die adoring God, loving my friends, not hating my enemies, and detesting superstition." This was dated and signed, and is preserved in the National Library at Paris. For a few days he seemed to recover from his illness. While in bed he corrected his *Irene,* added to it, and rewrote it in part. He arranged for actors and superintended the details of its production. He summoned strength enough to go to the theater.

Voltaire was always vain in his dress and personal appearance. He rode in a star-spangled coach, covered himself with a red coat lined with white ermine; he wore white stockings and silver buckles. He was small, lean and old. His nose, like a crow's beak, almost met his chin, but on his face was the everlasting smile. Through tumultuous crowds he drove to the Academy where he was received with wild acclamation— the Academy which had repeatedly refused to make him a member, but which now worshiped his genius and popularity. He spoke to the members, outlined a project for making a dictionary which is today the foundation of all the dictionaries of Europe.

He went to the theater to see his play. The building was crowded by a tumultuous, suffocating mob, representing all members of French society. Voltaire was hailed as a king. His bust was placed upon the stage; again and again they called for the old man to speak from the box. A laurel wreath was placed upon his head and the people went mad. When he left the theater the crowds went with him, following his carriage with shouts, and praise, and tears, until the old man reached his room. Voltaire himself wept like child: "If I had known the people would have committed such follies I would never have gone to the theater."

For a few days he seemed to regain his strength. He bought a house in Paris and determined to stay, but in May another attack seized him. The priest came to see him. Some say he made a confession, some say he refused it. Whether he did or not is of small importance. What he did in his dying hours, has nothing to do with the life he lived. One must be judged by his life and not by the agonies of death.

The life of Voltaire was so active and long that there can be no question of what it meant. Then, too, Voltaire knew that to be buried in consecrated ground, he must die with the benediction of the established church. All his life he had feared that he would be thrown in the gutter when dead. This was doubtless present in the old man's mind to the last. How he died it is impossible to tell. Some, that were with him, say he died in agony; some say he died in peace. The testimony of the witnesses depends largely upon their religious views. The papers were forbidden to notice his death, and the news was kept for a time from the people. On account of the testimony of the priest who said he had received absolution, and Voltaire's written confession of faith, he was accorded an honorable burial in consecrated ground at Romilly-on-Seine, 100 miles from Paris, the burial which all his life he desired. The next day a mandate was sent from the church forbidding that he be laid in consecrated ground, but he was already there.

Thirteen years later, by order of the National Assembly, which was then taking the first steps to overthrow the old regime and usher in the revolution, he was brought back to Paris. I cannot refrain from quoting here verbatim a short account of the return, written by that wonderful Englishwoman, Tallentyre, in her brilliant biography of Voltaire:

> On July 6th, 1791, a funeral car, decked with laurels and oak leaves, drawn by four horses and escorted by a detachment of the National Guard, left Romilly-on-Seine and began its solemn triumphal progress to Paris. On the front of the car was written, "To the memory of Voltaire." On one side, "If man is born free, he ought to govern himself!" on the other, "If man has tyrants, he ought to dethrone them."
> As it passed the villages, the people came out to greet it with wreaths of flowers and laurels in their hands. Mothers held up their babies that they, too, might say that they

had seen this great day; old men pressed forward to touch and be healed. At night the villages through which the procession passed were illuminated; by day could be seen triumphal arches, girls dressed in white and garlands of flowers. Out of their misery and wretchedness, the submerged poor recognized him who had wept and clamored for the right of all men and made freedom a possibility even for them.

At nightfall, on July 19th, the cortege reached Paris. The sarcophagus was placed on an altar on the ruins of that tower, of the Bastille in which Voltaire had been twice a prisoner.

On the altar was the inscription, "On this spot, where despotism chained thee, receive the homage of a free people."

All Sunday night the sarcophagus remined there. At three o'clock on the sunny afternoon of Monday, July 11th, it was placed on a car designed by David and drawn through Paris, escorted by an enormous company organized, orderly, and representing every rank and condition. Here were the men who had demolished the Bastille, carrying its flag, and in their midst that terrible virago who had led them in the fray. Here were citizens with pikes, Swiss, Jacobins, actors and soldiers. Some carried banners with devices from the dead man's writings. Some dressed in Greek costume, carried a gilt model of the famous statue by Houdin. Among the self-constituted guard were many who, not a month before, had brought back that other king to this capital—from Varennes—with howls, insults and imprecations.

Singers and music preceded the car itself. Supported on four great wheels of bronze, it looked like a magnificent altar. On the summit was the sarcophagus, and on that a full-length figure of Voltaire, reclining in an attitude of sleep and with a winged Immortality placing a crown of stars on his head.

The procession itself consisted of a hundred thousand persons. Six hundred thousand more witnessed it. It first stopped at the Opera House. The operatic company came forward and sang that song in Voltaire's *Samson,* which became, with the "Marseillaise," the song of the Revolution: "Wake ye people. Break your chains!"

After the Opera House, the Tuilleries was passed. Every window was filled with spectators, save one. Behind that, closed and barred, sat the most unhappy of mortals, Louis and Marie Antoinette, awaiting doom.

At last, at ten o'clock at night, and in a drizzling rain, the Pantheon was reached.

The sarcophagus was lifted into the place designed for it near the tombs of Descartes and Mirabeau.

In the Pantheon he reposed in peace until 1814. After the Revolution was over and the Bourbons returned to power, the tombs of both Voltaire and Rousseau were broken open. They were removed in a sack at night, taken to a place outside the city, emptied into a pit and consumed with quicklime. His ashes met the fate that he had dreaded all his life.

It is hardly necessary to sum up Voltaire. Born in a day of gross superstition, brutal barbarism, the densest bigotry and faith, he wrote his first play at the age of eighteen, and finished his last just before his death at eighty-four. During all this sixty-six years he worked unceasingly, dealing telling, deadly blows at the superstitions which held the minds of men. He died on the morning of the French Revolution, a revolution which more than any other man Voltaire inspired. Had he lived a few years longer most likely Voltaire would have died on the guillotine with many other victims of that delirious spasm of liberty that burned through France, and prepared the soil for a civilization and tolerance far greater than the world had ever known.

Voltaire was small in stature, lean and spare of figure, and active in body. His nimble mind was ever ablaze during all his life. Valiantly he fought on every intellectual battlefield. True he bowed and dodged and lied over and over again, that he still might live and work. Many of his admirers cannot forgive this in the great Voltaire. Rather they would have had him, like Bruno and Servetus, remain steadfast to his faith while his living body was consumed with flames. But, Voltaire was Voltaire, Bruno was Bruno, and Servetus was Servetus. It is not for the world to judge, but to crown them all alike. Each and all lived out their own being, did their work in their own way, and carried a reluctant, stupid humanity to greater possibilities and grander heights. Voltaire was emotional and kind; with a loving heart, a sensitive body, and imaginative mind. Voltaire marks the closing of an epoch. His life and his work stand between the old and the new. When he was cold, superstition had not yet died, but had received its mortal wound. Never again can savagery control the minds and thoughts of men. Never again can the prison thumbscrews and the rack be instruments to save men's souls. Among the illustrious heroes who have banished this sort of cruelty from the Western world no other name will stand so high and shine so bright as the illustrious name [of Voltaire].

5

The Skeleton in the Closet

The closet has so long been allotted to the skeleton that we have come to regard this room as its fit and natural home; it has been given over to this guest because it is the darkest, the closest and least conspicuous in the house. The door can be securely fastened and only now and then can the grating bones be heard by the world outside. Still, however, secluded and unused this guest chamber seems to be, and however carefully we bolt the door and darken every chink and crevice in the walls, we are ever conscious that the occupant is there, and will remain until the house is closed, and the last tenant has departed, never to return. The very fact that we try so hard to keep the skeleton in its proper room, makes it the more impossible to forget that it is there. Now and then we awake with a start at the thought of what might happen should it break the door and wander through the house, and then stray out into the wide world, and tell all the peaceful, trusting neighbors from what house it stole away; and yet we are somehow conscious that the rumor of its dread presence has already traveled as far as we are known. Man is a wonderfully adaptable animal; he fits himself easily into the environment where he is placed. He passes from infancy to childhood and from childhood to boyhood as smoothly as the placid river flows to the waiting sea. Every circumstance and surrounding of his life seems to have been made for him. Suddenly a new desire takes possession of his soul; he turns his back on the home of his childhood days and goes out alone. In a little time a new family is reared about him, and he forgets the group that clustered round his father's hearth. He may lose a leg or a fortune, and he soon conforms to his changed condition and life goes on as naturally and as easily as before. A child is born beneath his roof; it takes a place within his heart and home, and in a little while he can scarcely think of the day it was not there. Death comes, and a member of his little band is carried out, but time drops its healing balm upon the wounds and life goes on almost unconscious that the dead has ever lived. But while we adjust ourselves naturally to all things living and to ever varying scenes, the skeleton in the closet is always an intruder, no matter how long it may have dwelt beneath the roof. Even though we may forget its actual presence for a little time, still no scene is so perfect and no enjoyment so great but we feel a cloud casting its shadow across our happiness or the weight of some burden on our soul; and when we stop to ask the cause, the grinning skeleton reminds us that it is with us even here.

This spector stands quite apart from the other sorrows of our life; age seems powerless to forget, and time will not bring its ever-fresh, recurring scenes to erase the memory of the past. This is not because the skeleton is really such a dreadful guest. The kind and loving ivy creeps tenderly around each yawning scar and crumbling stone, until the whole ruin is covered with a lovely green. The decaying pile stands free and open to the sun and rain and air. It does not hide its head or apologize for the blemishes and seams that mark its face, and a kind, forgiving nature takes the ruin, scars and all, and blends these with her softening years and lovely face into a beautiful harmonious whole; but unlike the ruin, the skeleton in the closet is a neglected, outcast child. With every breath we insist that there is nothing in the room. We refuse to take it to our hearts and homes and acknowledge it as our own. We seek to strangle it to death, and each fresh attempt not only shows our murderous design, but proves that the skeleton is not a pulseless thing but is endowed with immortal life. The brighter the firelight that glows around our hearth, the more desolate and drear sounds the wail of the wind outside, for through its cold blasts wanders the outcast, whose rightful place is in the brightest corner of the room.

Our constant annoyance and sorrow at this dread presence is not caused by the way the skeleton behaves to us, but from the way we treat our guest. If we looked it squarely in its grinning skull, it might not seem so very loathsome to the sight. It has the right to grin. It may be but a grim smile over the consciousness that it has sounded the last sorrow and that henceforth no greater evils are in store; it may be a mocking, sardonic grin at the thought of our discomfiture over its unwelcome presence and the knowledge that we cannot drive it out.

There is no truer index to real character than the way we treat the skeletons with which we live. Some run to the closet door, and try to lock it fast when a neighbor comes their way. If perchance any fear of discovery is felt, they stand guard outside and solemnly protest that there is nothing in the room. Their anxiety and haste plainly show fear lest their hated guest shall reveal its face; and of course there rises in the neighbor's mind a vision of a skeleton more horrible by far than the one inside the door or than anyone can be. If the luckless jailer really fears that the rattle of the prisoner's bones has been heard outside, he feels it his duty to carefully explain or tediously cover up every detail and circumstance that caused the presence of the specter in the house. All this can only show that the guest is terrible to behold or that the jailer is so poor and weak that he himself is a helpless prisoner to his foolish pride and unmanly fear. It can only serve to emphasize the presence he tries so vainly to deny. There are also those who know that their skeleton has been seen, or who having lost all else but this persistent, grinning guest, drag it out and parade it in the world to gain the sympathy or the money of their neighbors and their friends, like the crippled beggar standing on the corner holding out his hat to every passer-by. The true man neither guiltily conceals nor anxiously explains nor vulgarly parades. He lives his life the best he can, and lets it stand for what it is. A thousand idle tales may be true or false. One may have seen but certain things, and placed him with the saints. Another little soul, who never felt the breadth and depth of human life, may have seen his scars alone, and cast him out. But standing by his side, or clasping his strong, sympathetic hand, no one thinks of halos or scars or asks an explanation of this or that, for in his whole being is felt the divine presence of a great soul, who has lived and loved, sinned and suffered, and been strengthened and purified by all.

The skeleton is really kind that it only grins as we look it in the face. Of all our household it has received the hardest treatment at our hands. It has helped us more than any of the rest, and been locked in the closet for its pains. It may perchance have come at our own invitation, bringing us the keenest, wildest joy our life had ever known. We gladly drained the pleasure to the dregs, and then coolly locked the memory close in the darkest hole that we could find. The day it came, has well nigh faded from our minds, and the mad, wild joy we knew can never more be awakened from the burned-out passions of the past, but the skeleton, which rose up grim and ghastly from the dying flame, remains to mock and jeer and make us sad. And now when the day is spent and the cup is drained, we charge the poor specter with our lasting pain, and forget the joy it brought. We look with dread at these mocking, grinning bones, which we cannot drive away, and we forget the time, long, long ago, when those dry sticks were covered up with beautiful and tempting flesh.

It may be that we shall always shudder as we hear the rattle of the bones when we pass the closet door, but in justice to the inmate, we should give him credit for the joys of long ago. And this brings us back to the old question of the balancing of pain and pleasure, good and evil, right and wrong. It may be that in the mysterious adjustment of nature's balances, a moment of supreme bliss will outweigh an eternity of pain. In the infinite economy, which life counted for the more,—that of Napoleon, or the poor French peasant that passed through an obscure existence to an unknown grave? The brief glory of Austerlitz was followed by the bitterness of Waterloo, and the long silence of an exile's life, while the peasant trod his short path without ambition, and filled a nameless grave without regret. Which is the greater and finer, the blameless life of the patient brute, or the winding, devious path of a human soul? It is only the dull level that brings no sorrow or regret. It is a sterile soil where no weeds will grow, and a bare closet where no skeleton will dwell.

Neither should we remember the skeleton only for the joy it brought; from the day it came, it has been the greatest benefactor that our life has known. When the mad delirium had passed away, and the last lingering fragrance was almost spent, this despised skeleton remained as the sole companion, whose presence should forever bind us back to those feelings that were fresh and true and straight from nature's heart, and that world which once was green and young and filled with pulsing life. As the shadows gather round our head, and our once-straying feet fall mechanically into the narrow path so straight and even at the farther end, we may shudder now and then at the thought of the grim skeleton whose life is so far removed from our sober later selves; but with the shudder comes a spark, a flash of that great, natural light and heat that once possessed this tottering frame, and gave a glow of feeling and a strength of purpose so deep and all-controlling that the artificial life of an artificial world seems no more than a dim candle shining by the glorious sun.

It is the exhausted emotions of age, which men call prudence, that are ever warning youth of the follies of its sins. It is the grinning skeleton, speaking truly from the memory of other days, that insists that life's morning held the halcyon hours. Does old age outlive the follies of childhood or does the man outgrow the wisdom of youth? The most vociferous preachers are often those whose natural spirits have led them to drink the deepest of life. They are so foolish as to think that others can be taught by their experiences, and mumbling greybeards endorse the excellence and wisdom of the sermons they preach. They are not wise enough to know that their prattle is more vain and foolish than the babblings of their childhood days. It was the growing, vital sap of life that made them children years ago; it is the icy, palsying touch of age that makes them babbling, preaching children once again. As well might the calm and placid lake teach the beauty of repose to the boiling, seething cataract that thunders down Niagara's gulf. When the troubled waters shall have reached the lake they shall be placid too. Nature is wiser far than man. She makes the first childhood precede the second. If the age of prudence came with youth, it would be a dull and prosy world for a little time; then life would be extinct upon the earth and death triumphant over all.

But these are the smallest reasons why we should venerate the neglected skeleton, which we have ruthlessly cast into the closet as if it were a hideous thing. This uncanny skeleton, ever thrusting its unwelcome bones into our presence and our lives, has been the most patient, persistent, constant teacher that all our years have known. We look backward through the long dim vista of the past, back to the little trusting child that once nestled on its mother's breast and from whose loving lips and gentle soul it first was a benediction to the life that was once a portion of herself. We remember still this mother's words teaching us the way to live and telling us the way to die. We always knew that no selfish thought inspired a single word she said and yet time and time again we strayed and wandered from the path she pointed out. We could not keep the road and after while we did not try. Again our teacher told us of the path. He, too, was good and kind and knew the way we ought to go, and showed us all the bad results of sin, and still we stumbled on. The preacher came and told us of the beauteous heaven, straight at the other end of the narrow path, and the yawning gulf of hell to which our shifting footsteps led; but we heeded not his solemn tones, though they seemed to come with the authority of God himself. As the years went on, our mother's voice was stilled, the teacher's words were hushed, the preacher's threats became an empty, hollow sound; and in their place came the grinning skeleton, born of our own desires and deeds; less loving than the gentle mother, more real and lifelike than the teacher, saner and truer than the preacher's idle words.

It was ever present and persistent; it was a portion of our very selves.

We detested and feared the hated thing; we locked it in the closet, and denied that it was there; but through the brightness of the day and the long and silent watches of the night, we heard its rattling bones, and felt its presence at our side. No teacher of our youth was like that grim and ghastly skeleton, which we tried to hide away. The schoolmaster of our early life took our fresh, young, plastic minds and sought to crowd them full of useless, unrelated facts that served no purpose through the years that were to come. These lessons that our teacher made us learn by rote filled so small a portion of our daily lives that most of them were forgotten when the schoolhouse door was closed. When now and then we found some use for a trifling thing that we had learned through years at school, we were surprised to know that the pedagogue had taught us even this. In those early days it seemed to us that life would consist of one long examination in which we should be asked the names of states, the rule of three, and the words the Romans used for this and that. All that we were taught of the great world outside and the problem that would one day try our souls, was learned from the copy books where we wrote the same old maxim until all the paper was used up. In after years, we learned that, while the copy book might have taught us how to write in a stilted, unused hand, still all its maxims were untrue.

We left school as ignorant of life as we commenced, nay, we might more easily have learned its lesson without the false, misleading theories we were taught were true. When the doors were opened and the wide world met us face to face, we tested what we learned, and found it false, and then we blundered on alone. We were taught by life that the fire and vigor of our younger years could not be governed by the platitudes of age. Nature was ever present with her strong and earthly grasp, her keen desires, her white hot flame. We learned the precepts of the books, but we lived the life that nature taught.

Our pathetic blunders and mistakes, and the skeleton that followed in their wake, remained to teach us what was false and point to what was true. This grim, persistent teacher made but little of the unimportant facts that the schoolmaster sought to make us learn, and it laughed to scorn the preacher's doctrine, that in some way we could avoid the results of our mistakes and sins. It did not preach, it took its place beside us as another self and by its presence sought to make us know that we could not be at peace until we clasped it to our breast and freely accepted the unwelcome thing as a portion of our lives.

Only the smallest fraction that we learned in youth was assimilated and made a portion of ourselves; the rest faded so completely that it seemed never to have been. The teacher soon became a dim, uncertain memory of the past, whose voice had long since died away; but the skeleton in the closet never wearied nor grew old. It ever made us learn again the lesson we would fain forget; opened at each succeeding period of our lives the pages we would gladly put away, until, at last, the ripening touch of time and the specter's constant presence made us know. From the day it came beneath our roof, it remained the liveliest, wisest, most persistent member of the family group, the tireless, watchful teacher, who would neither sleep nor allow its pupil to forget.

It may be that there are lives so barren and uneventful that this guest passes ever by their door, but unfortunate indeed is that abode where it will not dwell. The wide vistas can be seen only from the mountain top, and the infinite depths of life can be sounded only by the soul that has been softened and hallowed by the sanctifying touch of misery and sin.

Life is a never-ending school, and the really important lessons all tend to teach man his proper relation to the environment where he must live. With wild ambitions and desires untamed, we are spawned out into a shoreless sea of moving molecules of life, each separate atom journeying on an unknown course, regardless of the countless other lives it meets as it blindly rushes on; no lights nor headlands stand to point the proper way the voyager should take, he is left to sail an untried bar across an angry sea. If no disaster should befall, it does not show that the traveler is wise or good, but that his ambitions and desires are few or he has kept close inside the harbor line. At first we seek to swim the flood, to scale the rocky heights, to clutch the twinkling stars. Of course we fail and fall, and the scars our passions and ambitions leave, remain, though all our particles are made anew year after year. We learn at last to leave the stars to shine where they belong, to take all things as they are and adjust our lives to what must be.

The philosophy of life can come only from those experiences that leave lasting scares and results that will not die. Rather than seek to cover up these gaping wounds, we should accept with grace the tales they tell, and show them as trophies of the strife we have passed through. Those scars are honorable that have brought our lives into greater harmony with the universal power. For resist it as we will, this infinite loving presence will ever claim us as a portion of its self until our smallest fragments return once more to earth, and are united with the elements from which we came.

No life can be rounded and complete without the education that the skeleton alone can give. Until it came we never knew the capacities of the human soul. We had learned by rote to be forgiving, kind and true. But the anguish of the human soul cannot be told—it must be felt or never known. The charity born of true comradeship, which is the highest and holiest sentiment of life, can be taught by the skeleton alone. The self-righteous, who prate of forgiveness to their fellow men and who look down upon their sinning brothers from above, are hypocrites or fools. They either have not lived or else desire to pass for something they are not. No one can understand the devious, miry paths trodden by another soul unless he himself has wandered through the night.

Those placid, human lives that have moved along a narrow, even path; that learned by rote the lessons that the churches and the schools have ever taught; whose perfection consists in refraining from doing certain things in certain ways; who never had a noble thought or felt a great desire to help their fellow men—those blameless, aimless, worthless souls, are neither good nor bad. They neither feel nor think; no skeleton would deem it worth its while to come inside their door.

The world judges the conduct of youth by the standards of age. Even when due allowance is made for the inexperience and haste of the young, it is assumed that youth and age are measured by the calendar alone. Few have ever been wise enough to know that every passion and circumstance must be fully weighed, before an honest verdict can be written down; and that therefore only the infinite can judge a human soul.

Though accursed, doubted, and despised, Nature ever persists in her relentless plan. She would make us learn the lessons that youth so easily forgets. She finds us headstrong, unreasoning, and moved by the same feelings that sway the brute. She decrees that every act, however blind or willful, must leave its consequences on our lives, and these immortal consequences we treat as skeletons and lock them up. But these uncanny specters wrap us closely in their bony arms; they ever peer with sightless eyes into our soul; they are with us if we sleep or wake, and their persistent presence will not let us sleep. It is the hated, imprisoned skeleton that we vainly sought to hide away, that takes an untamed, fiery soul within its cruel, loving clasp, and holds it closely in its unforgiving grasp until the vain longings and wild desires of youth are subdued, and cooled, and the deep harmonies of life are learned. It is the hated skeleton that finds within our breast a heart of flint and takes this hard and pulseless thing and scars and twists and melts it in a thousand tortuous ways until the stony mass is purged and softened and is sensitive to every touch.

It is this same despised skeleton that finds us vain and boastful and critical of others' sins, that watches every word we speak and even each unuttered thought; it is with us when we tightly draw our robes and pass our fellow on the other side; it hears us when we seek to show how good we are by boasting of our neighbor's sins; for every spot of black or red that we see upon another's robes, it points its bony fingers to a scar upon our heart, to remind us that we are like the rest; and the same finger ever points us to our wounds until we feel and understand that the clay the Master used for us was as weak and poor as that from which he made the rest.

However blind and stubborn we may be, however long we deny the lesson that the skeleton would teach, still it will not let us go until with perfect peace and harmony we look at all the present and the past, at all that was, and all that is, and feel no regrets for what is gone, and no fears for what must come. It may be that our stubborn, stiff-necked soul will still persist until the hair is white and the heavy shoadows hang about our heads, but the skeleton with his soothing, softening ally, time, sits with the last watchers at our suffering bed, and goes if need be, to the silent grave, where alike the darkest crimson spot and the softest, purest clay are reunited once again with the loving, universal mother who has forgiven all and conquered all. It matters not how high we seem to climb, or what the careless world may think for good or ill. It matters not how many small ambitions we may seem to have achieved. Even the unworthy cannot be forever soothed by the hollow voice of fame. All triumphs are futile without the victory over self; and when the triumph over self is won, there are no more battles to be fought, for all the world is then at peace. It is the skeleton in the closet pointing ever to the mistakes and maladjustments of our past, the skeleton standing there before our gazes that makes us still remember where our lives fell short; that teaches us so slowly but so surely to turn from the unworthy victories and the dire defeats of life to the mastery of ourselves. It is the skeleton from whom we learn that we can live without the world, but not without ourselves.

Without the skeleton we could never feel another's sorrow, or know another's pain. Philosophy and theology cannot tell us how another's life became a hopeless wreck. It is ourselves alone that reveals the precipice along which every footpath leads. It is from life we learn that it is but an accident when we fall, and equally an accident when we keep the path. The pupil of the schools may look down with pitying glance upon the unfortunate victim of what seems to be his sin. He may point to a love that will forgive and kindly plead with him to take another path, but the wayfarer that the skeleton has taught will clasp this fellow mortal to his heart, for in his face he sees but the reflection of himself. The wise and good may forgive the evil and the wrong, but only the sinner knows that there is no sin.

The charity that is born of life and sin is not fine because of its effect on someone else, but for what it does for us. True charity is only the sense of the kinship of all living things. This is the charity that neither humiliates nor offends. It is the sense that brings a new meaning to life and a new purpose to the soul.

Let us do simple justice to this neglected, outcast guest, the useful, faithful teacher of our lives. Let us open the closet door, and let the skeleton come out, and lock the schoolmaster in its place. Let us leave this faithful friend to roam freely at its will. Let us look it squarely in the face with neither fear or shame, but with gratitude for the lessons it has taught. It may be that the jeering crowd will point in scorn as they see us with the gruesome figure at our side, but when we fully learn the lesson that it came to teach, we shall need to look no more without for the approval or disapproval of our acts, but seek to satisfy ourselves alone. Let us place a new chair beside the hearth, in the cosiest nook, and bid the skeleton take its place as the worthiest guest. Let us neither parade nor hide our new-found friend, but treat it as a fact of life—a fact that is, a fact that had the right to be, and a fact that taught us how to find ourselves. Let us not forget the parents who watch us in our youth, and the friends that were ever good and true. But above all, let us remember this grim and silent teacher, who never neglected or forgot, who showed us life as only it could show, who opened up new vistas to our soul, who touched our human hearts, who made us know and love our fellow man, who softened and mellowed and purified our souls until we felt the kinship that we bore to all living things. Until it came we knew only the surface of the world. Before it came, we had tasted of the shallow cup of joy and the bitter cup of pain, but we needed this to teach us from the anguish of the soul that there is a depth profound and great, where pain and pleasure both are one. That there is a life so deep and true that earth's rewards and penalties alike are but a hollow show; that there is a conquest of ourselves, which brings perfect peace and perfect rest.

PHILOSOPHY OF RELIGION

- ❑ Marcus Tullius Cicero—*The Nature of the Gods* and *On Divination*
- ❑ Ludwig Feuerbach—*The Essence of Christianity*
- ❑ David Hume—*Dialogues Concerning Natural Religion*
- ❑ John Locke—*A Letter Concerning Toleration*
- ❑ Lucretius—*On the Nature of Things*
- ❑ John Stuart Mill—*Three Essays on Religion*
- ❑ Friedrich Nietzsche—*The Antichrist*
- ❑ Thomas Paine—*The Age of Reason*
- ❑ Bertrand Russell—*Bertrand Russell On God and Religion* (edited by Al Seckel)

SOCIAL AND POLITICAL PHILOSOPHY

- ❑ Aristotle—*The Politics*
- ❑ Mikhail Bakunin—*The Basic Bakunin: Writings, 1869–1871*
  (translated and edited by Robert M. Cutler)
- ❑ Edmund Burke—*Reflections on the Revolution in France*
- ❑ John Dewey—*Freedom and Culture*
- ❑ John Dewey—*Individualism Old and New*
- ❑ John Dewey—*Liberalism and Social Action*
- ❑ G. W. F. Hegel—*The Philosophy of History*
- ❑ G. W. F. Hegel—*Philosophy of Right*
- ❑ Thomas Hobbes—*The Leviathan*
- ❑ Sidney Hook—*Paradoxes of Freedom*
- ❑ Sidney Hook—*Reason, Social Myths, and Democracy*
- ❑ John Locke—*Second Treatise on Civil Government*
- ❑ Niccolo Machiavelli—*The Prince*
- ❑ Karl Marx (with Friedrich Engels)—*The German Ideology*, including
  Theses on Feuerbach and *Introduction to the Critique of Political Economy*
- ❑ Karl Marx—*The Poverty of Philosophy*
- ❑ Karl Marx/Friedrich Engels—*The Economic and Philosophic Manuscripts of 1844*
  and *The Communist Manifesto*
- ❑ John Stuart Mill—*Considerations on Representative Government*
- ❑ John Stuart Mill—*On Liberty*
- ❑ John Stuart Mill—*On Socialism*
- ❑ John Stuart Mill—*The Subjection of Women*
- ❑ Friedrich Nietzsche—*Thus Spake Zarathustra*
- ❑ Thomas Paine—*Common Sense*
- ❑ Thomas Paine—*Rights of Man*
- ❑ Plato—*The Republic*
- ❑ Jean-Jacques Rousseau—*The Social Contract*
- ❑ Mary Wollstonecraft—*A Vindication of the Rights of Men*
- ❑ Mary Wollstonecraft—*A Vindication of the Rights of Women*

GREAT MINDS PAPERBACK SERIES

CRITICAL ESSAYS

- ❑ Desiderius Erasmus—*The Praise of Folly*
- ❑ Jonathan Swift—*A Modest Proposal and Other Satires*
  (with an introduction by George R. Levine)
- ❑ H. G. Wells—*The Conquest of Time* (with an introduction by Martin Gardner)

ECONOMICS

- ❑ Charlotte Perkins Gilman—*Women and Economics: A Study of the Economic Relation
  between Women and Men*
- ❑ John Maynard Keynes—*The General Theory of Employment, Interest, and Money*

- ❏ John Maynard Keynes—*A Tract on Monetary Reform*
- ❏ Thomas R. Malthus—*An Essay on the Principle of Population*
- ❏ Alfred Marshall—*Principles of Economics*
- ❏ Karl Marx—*Theories of Surplus Value*
- ❏ David Ricardo—*Principles of Political Economy and Taxation*
- ❏ Adam Smith—*Wealth of Nations*
- ❏ Thorstein Veblen—*Theory of the Leisure Class*

HISTORY

- ❏ Edward Gibbon—*On Christianity*
- ❏ Alexander Hamilton, John Jay, and James Madison—*The Federalist*
- ❏ Herodotus—*The History*
- ❏ Charles Mackay—*Extraordinary Popular Delusions and the Madness of Crowds*
- ❏ Thucydides—*History of the Peloponnesian War*
- ❏ Andrew D. White—*A History of the Warfare of Science with Theology in Christendom*

LAW

- ❏ John Austin—*The Province of Jurisprudence Determined*

PSYCHOLOGY

- ❏ Sigmund Freud—*Totem and Taboo*

RELIGION

- ❏ Thomas Henry Huxley—*Agnosticism and Christianity and Other Essays*
- ❏ Ernest Renan—*The Life of Jesus*
- ❏ Upton Sinclair—*The Profits of Religion*
- ❏ Elizabeth Cady Stanton—*The Woman's Bible*
- ❏ Voltaire—*A Treatise on Toleration and Other Essays*

SCIENCE

- ❏ Nicolaus Copernicus—*On the Revolutions of Heavenly Spheres*
- ❏ Charles Darwin—*The Autobiography of Charles Darwin*
- ❏ Charles Darwin—*The Descent of Man*
- ❏ Charles Darwin—*The Origin of Species*
- ❏ Charles Darwin—*The Voyage of the Beagle*
- ❏ Albert Einstein—*Relativity*
- ❏ Michael Faraday—*The Forces of Matter*
- ❏ Galileo Galilei—*Dialogues Concerning Two New Sciences*
- ❏ Ernst Haeckel—*The Riddle of the Universe*
- ❏ William Harvey—*On the Motion of the Heart and Blood in Animals*
- ❏ Werner Heisenberg—*Physics and Philosophy: The Revolution in Modern Science* (introduction by F. S. C. Northrop)
- ❏ Julian Huxley—*Evolutionary Humanism*
- ❏ Edward Jenner—*Vaccination against Smallpox*
- ❏ Johannes Kepler—*Epitome of Copernican Astronomy* and *Harmonies of the World*
- ❏ Isaac Newton—*The Principia*
- ❏ Louis Pasteur and Joseph Lister—*Germ Theory and Its Application to Medicine* and *On the Antiseptic Principle of the Practice of Surgery*
- ❏ Alfred Russel Wallace—*Island Life*

SOCIOLOGY

- ❏ Emile Durkheim—*Ethics and the Sociology of Morals* (translated with an introduction by Robert T. Hall)